The Road to Audacity

THE ROAD TO
AUDACITY

Being Adventurous in Life and Work

Stephen Carter
Jeremy Kourdi

palgrave
macmillan

First published 2003 by
PALGRAVE MACMILLAN
Houndmills, Basingstoke, Hampshire RG21 6XS and
175 Fifth Avenue, New York, N.Y. 10010
Companies and representatives throughout the world

PALGRAVE MACMILLAN is the global academic imprint of the Palgrave
Macmillan division of St. Martin's Press, LLC and of Palgrave Macmillan Ltd.
Macmillan® is a registered trademark in the United States, United Kingdom
and other countries. Palgrave is a registered trademark in the European
Union and other countries.

ISBN 1–4039–0617–3

This book is printed on paper suitable for recycling and made from fully
managed and sustained forest sources.

A catalogue record for this book is available from the British Library.

Library of Congress Cataloging-in-Publication Data

Carter, Stephen.
  The road to audacity : being adventurous in life and work / by Stephen
Carter and Jeremy Kourdi.
      p. cm.
Includes bibliographical references and index.
   ISBN 1–4039–0617–3 (cloth)
   1. Organizational behavior. 2. Psychology, Industrial 3. Risk-taking
(Psychology) I. Kourdi, Jeremy. II. Title.

HD58.7 .C354 2003
   650.1—dc22

                                                2003055267

Editing and origination by Aardvark Editorial, Mendham, Suffolk

10   9   8   7   6   5   4   3   2   1
12 11 10 09 08 07 06 05 04 03

Printed and bound in Great Britain by
Creative Print & Design (Wales), Ebbw Vale

Contents

LIST OF FIGURES AND TABLES

Figures

Tables

It all started when the senior manager of a very large business decided he wanted his company to be more audacious and someone thought we might be able to help.

My first impulse on seeking to help was to round up the usual suspects – the great and good of corporate life regularly eulogised in print – and then I hesitated. What exactly was audacity and why would the leader of a successful business want more of it? And, short of offering a list of distinguished and not so distinguished role models, exactly how was someone or some corporation to develop it?

The more I delved the more it seemed I was asking a question where the answers were not going to come from the standard sources. And so it became a puzzle and, I suppose, a bit of a quest. Trying to answer these questions became an adventure undertaken for itself, although since then all sorts of results and outcomes have been achieved.

To search for the road to audacity meant starting in and travelling through some novel places. On this quest some people have provided some very useful signposts and bearings. Foremost among these has been the work and friendship of Michael J. Apter, creator of reversal theory and in my opinion one of the great psychologists of the past few decades. Reversal theory is quite simply the most powerful account of what it is to be human that I have come across and one that particularly talks the spirit of audacity. I have really wanted to capture the insights it has given me and hopefully communicate them to a wider audience. Mike's enthusiasm for this project and his willingness to consider new dimensions to the implications and expansion of the theory are an example of the generosity of a great mind.

Spending time over an eighteen-month period working and drinking a few beers occasionally with Steve Venables, the British mountaineer and writer, raised my curiosity about the spark that makes some of us climb out of the valley and pastures and up into the peaks. His ability to articulate and communicate the compulsion of this was an inspiration and led me into areas of human experience of which, as a lesser motal, I had been ignorant. In this vein the energy and friendship of Barry Roberts has also been superb, together with his rather quixotic attempts to render me fitter and more able to survive in the great outdoors.

On the route to a finished book, a travelling companion can be a boon. The last book I had written – *Renaissance Management* – had taken me over two years to write and I really couldn't conceive of committing to a similar lengthy project. What I needed was a colleague to help keep the speed up and contribute in lots of ways. Jeremy Kourdi I knew would be the perfect foil and so it proved. He is a most generous writing partner, always positive and enthusiastic, supportive of new ideas, patient in dealing with my somewhat erratic typing, grammar and sentence construction, full of good examples, case studies and intelligent insight and he has a great sense of readability. To spare his blushes, most of the anecdotes in the first person singular are mine and were retained as it was felt that they helped to make some of the ideas in the book more immediate. To not spare his blushes, the particular story about being harassed by a penis extension electronic salesman is most definitely his.

Many other people have contributed to this book, both directly and indirectly. My colleagues Marie Shelton and Mitzi Desselles are a constant source of criticism, support, challenge, friendship and unbelievable tolerance. My debt to them is great, as it is to Andrew Kerry of the Boots Company. It was his audacious determination that enabled the leadership programme in the Alps, described later in the book, to happen instead of remaining a pipe dream. As a result this meant that we could explore how to make many of the ideas in this book real and practical.

In trying to create a new way of looking at the challenge of audacity, Jeremy and I are also grateful to those who helped us go into what was, for us, undiscovered territory. In particular we should mention Phillip White-head MEP who always makes time to help and advise, Graham Mackay CEO of SABMiller, Steve Barrow and his colleagues at HSBC and Dr Gene Crozier of the Chartered Management Institute. Richard Davies, also of SABMiller, has been a tremendous support and help, as was his colleague Mandy Roussouw.

Without wishing to sound trite, if making this book was a journey, thank you and love to Sharon, Sara, Samantha, Lucy-Jane and Jack, for being at home to come back to.

Finally, some of the ideas in this book are not the responsibility of any of the above, even Jeremy. For all that is muddled, wrong-headed or simply mistaken, please blame me.

STEVE CARTER

The Road to Audacity is the result of the support and encouragement of many people, and their expertise must be acknowledged. First, Steve Carter – this book was his idea and his originality, insight, generosity and good humour made travelling the road to audacity immensely rewarding and great fun. We were very fortunate to work with an excellent editor at Palgrave Macmillan, Stephen Rutt, and his talented team whose patience and energy is much appreciated. I would also like to thank those friends and many colleagues who I have worked with over the years and who have, without doubt, provided the most intelligent, stimulating and innovative opportunities to learn and develop.

Finally, my gratitude goes, as always, to my family, Julie, Thomas and Louise, who have not only provided constant encouragement, but also thought-provoking opinions and the inspiration to write.

JEREMY KOURDI

What is Audacity?

Audacity is – what? It involves courage, boldness, achievement, but it is more than that. It is a complex idea with a cultural perspective. An American friend questioned the use of it, saying that as a child she would hear her mother reprimand her, crying: 'You had the *audacity* to do that!'

It seems to include an aspect of rule-breaking – it is not just a synonym for being brave – but it also seems to include a sense of wilfulness, non-conformity, deliberate failure to meet expectations. From the viewpoint of my friend's mum, it could be seen to be an act of rudeness or defiance.

Just what an organisation needs: mischief and rule-breaking.

At this point, I can imagine one or two people putting this book gently in the sand bucket and calling the emergency services. Surely organisations, in fact society as a whole, need rules to follow, certainty to prevail and expectations to be met? Is it not the case that there is enough mischief in the world? The last thing you want, I hear a hundred managers saying, is 'people going off at a tangent', making it up for themselves, fixing things that aren't broken.

True.

Yet in almost any society and in almost any organisation there will be stories and examples of rules being broken, expectations ignored or protocol defied, directly leading to great success, the business transformed, society renewed. We often make heroes of those who rebelled against conventional wisdom and advice. For example, James Dyson in the UK bucked the trend and prevailing wisdom to launch a new white goods manufacturing business that is now extremely successful, *despite* the advice he got from everyone that it was impossible. Science provides particularly stark reminders of how individuals can question existing orthodoxy and lead us to some startling discoveries, often in the face of hostile criticism and challenges. Whether it is Galileo insisting that the world is round and defying the Pope; Einstein challenging Newtonian views of gravity that had prevailed for over two centuries to produce his General Theory of Relativity, or Watson and Crick explaining how DNA is structured in a double helix, it can be argued that we are at our very best when we question, challenge and rebel.

Clearly, there is such a thing as good mischief. Why is this?

Journeys and destinations

Expectations are like maps: they provide signposts for where to go and what to do. In an uncertain territory, whether it be technological, market or literal, a map is a source of certainty and reassurance.

I was once told the tale of a party of walkers who got lost in the wilderness of the Scottish Highlands. The weather closed in and the situation grew desperate. People started to worry. 'Never fear', said the leader, 'I have a map.' Reassured, the party carried on in good heart, eventually finding a road and the warmth and safety of a Scottish pub. There the leader admitted that the map he had was in fact one of the English Lake District! The story was told as an example of good leadership – providing everyone with the comfort of a sense of direction.

'Lucky devil!' was my thought when I heard this tale. I think sometimes that it is important to admit that there isn't a map and that following the wrong one is simply crazy. At times, what is required is to acknowledge we are travelling in uncharted territory – there is no map. None of us have been here before and we are working out a new route. To map lovers this is certainly mischievous, but it is more realistic. There may be a whiff of rebellion about ignoring the map, but going into the unknown may require it. Undoubtedly, maps and expectations have a purpose – sometimes paradoxically, as a reference point for departing from them.

The idea of pioneering a new route and the tale of the lost walkers suggest another aspect to audacity: it seems to be about the results *and* the means by which they are achieved. Maintaining the metaphor, audacity involves both the destination and the journey. An organisation that achieves great results by tried and tested means would probably not be called audacious. Nor will one that tries out new ideas and yet never achieves anything; failed, probably, but audacious?

Moreover, audacity seems to imply there is excitement, even exhilaration, to be gained and that the means is something worthwhile in itself.

Seeking new experiences rather than just new goals is at the heart of what it is to be human: curiosity provides its own reward. It is a special kind of experiment in which nothing is necessarily proven but something is always found out. How often have you found when someone has been asked why they did something that their response is quizzical: 'to find out if I could', 'to see what it was like', 'to learn something about myself.'

Wilfred Thesiger, crossing and recrossing the Empty Quarter, the unforgiving desert within a desert in Southern Arabia, typified this attitude:

> He loved the harsh emptiness of the slow-moving waves of the sand dunes and the bleak plains of sun-blasted salt flats. He was challenged by the prospect of crossing regions where no white man had been before, not so much for scientific discovery or research but for the pure adventure. But having crossed it once he came back to it again by another route, and then again and again, just to live and travel with the Bedu whose lifestyle he admired and enjoyed so much.[1]

Some businesses seem innately curious. They are organisations that can reinvent themselves. Exploring is written into their culture. They go far beyond the goal-setting destination focus of other businesses. They are organisations that seem to be enjoying themselves. For them, we can argue, the destination sometimes can become the servant of the journey.

This happy band

In principle, I am wary of drawing parallels from myth and legend to the running of organisations. Management literature is full enough of fiction without imposing any more. However, one cannot help but be struck by how reflecting upon audacity leads one to notice the echoes of the ancient stories of the past – particularly the many heroic tales about journeys involving a close-knit band following a leader whose purpose is to do something dangerous and different, facing uncertainty and hidden perils. From the tales of *Odysseus*, through *The Pilgrim's Progress* to *The Lord of the Rings*, there seems to be a common theme of a close-knit band of individuals taking on the odds. Mastering new problems and threats, the band can often bring together individuals with personal strengths or special skills vital to the expedition.

We would probably want to call these epics 'audacious', and wonder why Frodo and his friends don't do the sensible thing and stay in the warmth of their hobbit hole. Audacity brings people together in a common cause, whether that be sporting, organisational, plain adventurism or something more profound. As we shall see, this band provides a kind of protection, a way of dealing with the world that helps make us face uncertainty with greater confidence and enjoy the danger.

I remember in my early twenties being three thousand miles from home, travelling on a bus ticket in a direction that would take me another two thousand miles from home to a destination in which I would have no money, no return ticket and no work. Not surprisingly, I suppose, I felt alone and unhappy. Somewhere in the middle of the night, changing buses, I fell in with two others also journeying into a personal unknown. All of a sudden I had companions! All of a sudden, the wide open spaces, unfamiliar sights and even downtown terminals seemed exciting again. All of a sudden, the unfamiliar was a friend. The strange thing, of course, was that materially the odds had not changed – still no job, money or means of return.

And, of course, my companions eventually got off the bus.

Typically in these tales there is a point at which the leader and perhaps some of the band face a moment of test or truth alone, a moment in which all may be lost – materially, physically or morally. Time and again in writing this book we have come across examples where no matter how loyal and committed a group of people are audacity, in the end, will boil down to a lonely moment of truth. This can be the climber who decides to press on alone when others are forced to turn back. It can be the scientist who publishes a radical hypothesis knowing it will inflame established orthodoxy. This can be the (real) manager of a major corporation who, continually blocked by his boss over something he felt was critical to the company, put it simply to his adversary, saying: 'Back this, or I will go to *your* boss and resign, telling him why.'

For him there were moments when, if you wanted to achieve anything, you had to be prepared to die for it.

Dying here would have been metaphorical, and often the risk can be little more than embarrassment or loss of face. We recover. In other instances, sacrifice can be literal. In Phillip Whitehead's memorable phrase: 'Each night, Robert Kennedy and Martin Luther-King made their speeches looking down the barrel of a gun.'

Being audacious is a curiously rich mixture of ideas, somewhat paradoxical in its nature. As we have seen, it involves:

- A destination and a journey.
- A map and a wilful step into the unknown.
- A struggle and relationships that endure.
- A personal challenge and a band of fellow travellers.

Organisations and individuals that seek to be audacious in order to thrive in an uncertain world are embarking on a form of development that is about mindset and values, and at the end of which the world will look utterly different. We shall see in Chapter 1 that uncertainty and risk are not to be tamed by calculation and prediction. Its basis is provided by our perceptions and psychology. Certainly, we will always try and manage the odds unless we are bent on self-destruction, but unless we are prepared to change ourselves, we are doomed to travel the easier and less rewarding path.

Note

I   Bonnington, C. (1971) *Quest for Adventure*, Hodder & Stoughton, London

CHAPTER ONE

The Road to Audacity

As we write this book (March 2003), our country is at war, and no one knows how it will end. A deadly new virus is gripping the peoples of Asia and other places, with no known cure. The world's leading stock markets have fallen by over 40 per cent in the last two years. Recently, one of the country's leading economists explained that he could not see where significant improvements would come from in the next two years. Changes in the world's climate continue to alarm many scientists. (By the time you read this book, you will know perhaps how one or two things turned out, but you will also be deep in a new set of uncertainties.)

These, one might fairly say, are uncertain times.

Despite these situations, this book is no counsel of despair. Instead, it is a guide to using the audacious character in all of us to cope better with uncertainty and respond more effectively to it at an individual and organisational level.

The call to be audacious and adventurous is something that inspires all of us at some time – even if we quickly submerge it when we consider the implications for our comfort and security. However, it just may be that to be more successful the call needs to be heeded. Many individuals and organisations are becoming aware that the old certainties of the past are crumbling and a more volatile future requiring a more adventurous spirit is emerging. This book will help you consider *why* we need to be more audacious, and *how* we can go about promoting this in our organisations and ourselves. Above all, it is firmly based on the belief that audacity is for everyone, not simply the domain of a few.

Living in a clockwork world?

Painful though it is to politicians, business leaders and the armchair critic in all of us, we do not live in a clockwork world. We are discovering that the efforts of the last century to create certainty and predictability in all aspects of life seem to be unravelling. The repetition of the production line, the quality process and the great political movements, with their appeal to rationality and reasonableness, do not hold the promise they once did. It is perhaps ironic that at a time when human knowledge, discovery and insight have never been greater or more widely shared, the biggest discovery of all is how much we do *not* know.

There is much that we are uncertain about, probably most things. This uncertainty exists at every level: society, organisations, teams and individuals. We fool ourselves if we believe otherwise. John Adams, an important theorist of risk, has remarked:

> Virtually all formal treatments of risk and uncertainty in game theory, operations research, economics or management science require that the odds be known, that numbers be attached to probabilities and magnitudes of possible outcomes. In practice, since such numbers are rarely available, they are assumed or invented, the alternative being to admit that the formal treatments have nothing useful to say about the problem under discussion.[1]

Although there are problems where the odds are either known or calculable, these are trivial in comparison with problems posed by uncertainty. According to Adams, 'This is the realm not of calculation but of judgement.'

Adams is highlighting one of the issues that make understanding and managing risk so very difficult: the sheer complexity of reality. However, the answer to succeeding in a world of exhausting change and uncertainty is clear: it is to take risks that pay off. Crucially, as well as potentially leading to a successful outcome, travelling along this road also provides an exciting, fulfilling and motivational journey. To an extent, audacity is a self-reinforcing mechanism: audacity leads to motivational fulfilment, which in turn raises the likelihood of success. After all, motivated people tend to be more assured and successful than people feeling frustration, buffeted by uncertainty and searching – possibly in vain – for familiarity.

This book will provide a guide to following a more adventurous and ultimately successful journey: the road to audacity.

In making this journey we need to explore the relationship between three factors: uncertainty, risk and audacity. Uncertainty means not knowing the likelihood or nature of a number of possible future events, whereas typically risk relates to the probability of one particular outcome occurring. Audacity is the human factor or mindset determining which course of action we take in relation to that probability. As has already been suggested by Adams, the first two components are much more blurred than we like to think they are. Not being able to distinguish in reality between uncertainty and risk emphasises the third factor – audacity – as a key determinant of how individuals and organisations behave in an uncertain world. For the rest of this book, when we refer to risk we mean the uncertain likelihood of events to which we might audaciously respond or not.

Why risk it? The value of risk-taking and audacity

At the heart of any business or enterprise is the capacity to take risks. To succeed in this we need to be audacious.

Capitalism works on the simple basis of competition. It requires a product to be better than or preferable to its competitors. It involves anticipating the responses of a changing and perhaps even fickle market that may not know what it wants until it appears. If the market was certain and regulated, theory and practice suggests that it would inevitably become inefficient and wasteful.

Organisations have managed the excitement out of risk. Increasingly, risk is seen as being negative, something to be avoided, skirted around, assiduously managed, minimised or removed altogether. When we discuss risk, it is invariably with a wary sense of concern, even alarm that has long been bred into us. Being audacious and prepared to take risks is counterintuitive – the trend is for organisations to seek certainty and actively avoid risk.

Furthermore, society teaches us as individuals to approach risk with caution and concern. The alternative is seen as gambling, an undesirable vice, and risk is seldom welcomed as an opportunity. This view of risk as bad is simplistic: it fails to take account of the value of risk, that it can represent opportunity and, most importantly, that we need the excitement that comes with risk to perform at our best. Given such ingrained attitudes it is useful to highlight the value of audacity and risk-taking.

The commercial case for risk

Audacity in the commercial arena is an issue that presents both a carrot and stick: the carrot is the prospect of exploiting scarcity, doing something that commands a profitable, secure market position. The stick is the danger of doing nothing, or worse, mishandling the risks that surround us in a way that brings failure. If we succeed in being audacious then we can start a virtuous circle by learning from our success, building confidence and making progress. If we ignore risk, mishandle it or fail to be audacious, then a vicious spiral can result. Risk is resented, rued and avoided; confidence and the ability to effectively handle risk are reduced. Often, we simply don't know what to do, and may do too little or too much. Failure can pile upon failure, with any risk being seen as a grim harbinger of doom, rather than a potential opportunity.

The economic and commercial importance of risk is clear, although rarely made explicit (unlike the situation with individual risk). Firms create value and generate profits when their product offer has an element of scarcity, meaning that it provides something of value that is not readily available elsewhere. Cult products do this by making something unique, which only the initiated can buy. The publisher Bloomsbury goes even further than this with the Harry Potter novels by emphasising their complete *unavailability* before a certain date. However, closely linked with scarcity is the issue of risk. Usually, developing scarcity means going further, spending more or in some other way being different from what has gone before. For example, this may mean a mobile phone network investing in new infrastructure, an aircraft manufacturer developing a new plane, a shop opening a new branch or entering a new market – the scope of risk is almost without end.

Now here is the crucial point: the more significant the decision, meaning the greater the chance of achieving scarcity and creating greater value, the larger the risk. This fact is recognised in many of our commercial structures and practices such as banking, investing and insurance. The competitive nature of commerce means that all economic activity carries a risk. Competitors – whether actual or potential – pose a sustained and permanent risk. If we are cowed by the presence of risk or if we act out of fear, then the result may well be decisions that are rash, inferior and flawed.

To illustrate the importance of audacity in business, consider the remarkable success story of Swatch's market entry. In the 1980s, the Swiss watch industry was at a crossroads. For many years, it had enjoyed a reputation for premium quality but it had been surrendering the popular, low-cost end of the market to Japanese companies. These businesses were using their enviable reputation for technology, engineering and reliable low-cost production gained in other products (from cars to domestic appliances) and were squeezing the Swiss watch industry into an ever diminishing niche at the top end of the market. (Interestingly, technology was causing this end of the market to shrink, as customers were buying Swiss watches that lasted for life and could even be passed on as heirlooms.) The Swiss, who had been market leaders for as long as anyone could remember, now found their expertise was counting against them: they were perceived as being out of touch and outmoded in the age of mass quartz crystal chronometers.

With an aggressive and imaginative campaign, the Swiss moved to retake the industry that they had dominated for so long. Swatch launched a range of stylish watches aimed at a youthful mass market. Its comprehensive and sophisticated campaign involved massive media advertising, promotions and sponsorship events, and caught the public imagination. Swatch styling has since been applied to other industries. For example, when Daimler entered the market for urban runabout cars it collaborated with Swatch, developing the Smart car. The car may have met with a mixed reception but the position of Swatch as a fashion icon is assured.

Swatch has been successful and, unusually for a single firm, has helped to redefine the market. For example, there are now watches for sports use, leisurewear and executives as well as traditional styles. Among the reasons for Swatch's success was an audacious, wilful approach that threw away the rule-book, understanding the changing market and attempting to lead it. Interestingly, if Swatch described its plans and produced prototypes ahead of launch it may have been ridiculed, but by understanding who it was targeting – younger, sporty people looking for style and reliability – and aggressively marketing its concept, this became one of the greatest market entries ever.

With the need both to add value for customers and differentiate products comes risk. Commercial advantage rarely resides in an easy, well-trodden domain of certainty; rather, it lies in the much more complex and challenging world of risk.

Risk and the individual

Risk is valuable for many reasons: commercial, economic and above all, individual. Risk-taking is essentially a part of who we are. It connects very closely to our basic value of freedom. Many people claim they are afraid of moving jobs, becoming self-employed, changing relationships or moving locations, for example. This concern is often real, deep, significant, and yet it is frequently dismissed or shrugged off. It may seem to over-emphasise the issue, yet many people feel trapped, often because of inertia or a fear of the unknown. Implicit in this is the risk of change and the uncertainty inherent in new or challenging situations. The ability to successfully take a risk leading to personal, individual change (such as a career move) is the key to learning, to developing personal skills and abilities – in short, to achieving progress. In this sense, risk has a significant individual value. Yet risk-taking is often regarded as unusual at best, and at times foolish or reckless.

Risk is an intensely personal phenomenon, with our attitudes to it shaped by our experiences, confidence and abilities – in short, by the nature of who we are. This is a two-way street. Not only does risk affect how we act, but also how we act in a risky situation (the extent that we are audacious) invariably determines how far and fast we can progress.

Driven to audacity – the case of Chrysler

There are many examples of commercial risks that have paid off. One case – that of Bob Lutz and the renaissance of Chrysler – highlights particularly well the value of being audacious commercially. During the late 1980s, Chrysler found sales in the USA and abroad weakening; critics claimed the organisation was uninspired and lagging behind its competitors. Each problem was seen as unique and people tackled them separately, whereas they were really symptoms of a larger problem facing the whole company. The solution for Chrysler was to see the bigger picture, thus rescuing the company's fortunes. Bob Lutz, the company's President, believed the answer was to develop an innovative, exciting car. Stylish, with a powerful ten-cylinder engine and five-speed manual transmission, the Dodge Viper was given a premium price of US$50,000. Many colleagues pointed out that no US-made car would sell in volume at that price, and that the investment would be better spent elsewhere. Lutz's idea was based on nothing more than personal instinct, without any significant market research. He had to overcome considerable internal opposition as this approach to decision-making was not typical at Chrysler. However, the Dodge Viper was a massive commercial success. It changed the public's perception of Chrysler, halted the company's decline and boosted morale.

Bob Lutz's belief that the radically different Dodge Viper was the right decision for Chrysler has been hailed as a triumph of instinct over rationality. In truth, both elements were present, both instinct and experience. When threatened with stagnating sales, a lacklustre brand and competitive pressures, Lutz's response was to throw away the rule-book, innovate and do something radically different to connect with customers. In short, to be audacious.

The inevitability of risk

So far we have highlighted the value of taking risks to organisations and individuals – but do they actually have a choice? Organisations do not exist by right: their fortunes depend on how effectively they adapt to change, uncertainty and the risk that invariably follows. The concept of the *volatility curve* (Figure 1.1) makes a very simple proposition: that the greater the level of change and renewal in an organisation's operating environment, the less easy it becomes to exercise rigid top-down control. The result is greater pressure for a structure and style centred upon individual action, and informal, looser operating arrangements.

In operating environments and markets where there is low volatility, repeatability and economies of scale are the dominant management concerns. These are best achieved by rigid specification and viewing employees as 'holders of roles', carrying out tasks and implementing decisions that have been made elsewhere. This is very much the environment of mass production of the twentieth century in which total control of every aspect of the supply chain was viewed as achievable and desirable. It was on this basis that many of the world's large corporations grew and formed their distinctive contribution to human history.

It is no news, however, that the world is changing, in particular, the world of organisations where the impact of information technology has, almost without exception, left every industry facing fundamental shifts in the way successful organisations operate. The impact of this is felt in every aspect of organisational life.

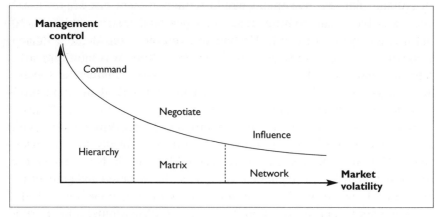

Figure 1.1 Management control and market volatility

Source: Carter, S. (1999) *Renaissance Management*, Kogan Page

At the core of this change has been the need for organisations to re-evaluate the way they view and manage their employees. High levels of change mean that decision-making is increasingly dispersed throughout the organisation as it struggles to keep up with the rate of change. Employees, instead of waiting to be told what to do, increasingly need to respond and proactively control events themselves. Top management is simply not in a position either to understand the nature of this pressure or to be able to respond quickly enough. Business life is therefore becoming more uncertain, as greater levels of volatility affect more people.

More junior managers are used to senior colleagues taking the uncertainty out of their lives by giving them clear instructions on what to do. Current complexity, information and the pace of change mean that this is no longer possible – what is required is greater willingness to take risks and to let other people take risks at all levels of the organisation.

Handling uncertainty

So by choice or necessity, how do we deal with risk? Not surprisingly, given shareholder expectations, competitive pressures and market volatility, organisations and the individuals within them have a huge desire to control uncertainty, to tame it, to make it theirs. There is a strong need to believe that if we could understand the odds we can select the right strategy and succeed. (Of course, many individuals and organisations do not think about risk at all, hoping instead that it will go away.) However, in pursuit of the need to control the odds and select the right strategy, organisations typically categorise risk in the ways described in Table 1.1.

What is interesting about this list is that it seeks to reduce uncertainty by not addressing the risk of *opportunities not taken*. Yet this is precisely where some of the most dangerous risks are. One of the most successful Internet businesses in the UK is Freeserve, an Internet Service Provider that was massively rewarding for its parent company, Dixon's, before it was sold off. We know of a senior executive in a famous UK company who had also spotted this as a major opportunity but could not get backing for it – an organisation currently having a torrid time trying to work out its future. On a personal level, we once worked with a talented manager who had failed, over many years, to embrace risk, preferring instead the comfortable, formalised life that he believed that his talent and effort deserved. As he approached retirement, he felt a deep sense of frustration that his experience and ability were not recognised and better rewarded – one suspects that he never felt fulfilled.

Table 1.1 Areas of organisational risk				
Financial	**Commercial**	**Strategic**	**Technical**	**Operational**
Accounting decisions and practices	Loss of key personnel and tacit knowledge	Marketing, pricing and market entry decisions	Failure of plant or equipment	Product or design failure, including failure to maintain supply
Treasury risks	Failure of commercial partners (such as licensees, agents, JV partners)	Acquisitions decisions	Infrastructure failure	Failure to develop new products
Financial viability of debtors and strategic suppliers	Failure to comply with legal regulations or codes of practice	Market changes affecting commercial decisions (due to customers and/or competitors)	Accidental or negligent actions (such as fire, pollution, floods)	Client failure
Fraud	Contract conditions	Political or regulatory developments		Breakdown in labour relations
Robustness of information management systems	Poor brand management or handling of a crisis	Resource-building and resource allocation decisions		Corporate malpractice (such as sex discrimination)
Inefficient cash management	Market changes			Political change
Inadequate insurance				

This seems to be an odd way of looking at risk. It seems to be all about avoidance. The risk of failure implies a mindset that is not the same as that of the risk of not succeeding.

So, typically organisations see risk as something to be mitigated or avoided, highlighting not only *where* things might go wrong and *what* their impact would be, but *how*, *why* and *where* they might be triggered. They recognise five potential risk catalysts:

Technology

New hardware, software or system configurations can trigger risks, as well as new demands placed on existing information systems and technology.

Organisational change

Risks are triggered by issues such as new management structures or reporting lines, new strategies and commercial agreements (including mergers, agency or distribution agreements).

Processes
New products, markets and acquisitions all cause process change, and this in turn can trigger risks to occur.

People
New personnel, a loss of key people or poor succession planning can all lead to dislocation. However, the main cause of dislocation within this category is people's behaviour: everything from laziness to fraud, exhaustion to simple human error and many factors besides, can be a catalyst, resulting in risk being realised.

External environmental factors
Changes such as regulation, political, economic or social developments can all severely affect strategic decisions, bringing to the surface risks that may have lain hidden. Because each risk may have a different level of impact and consequence, quantifying their effects, even in the most general of terms, is deemed essential. The risks in each of the categories mentioned are mapped both in terms of likely frequency and potential impact, with the emphasis on materiality. In fact, risks can even be mapped on a 2×2 matrix (Figure 1.2).

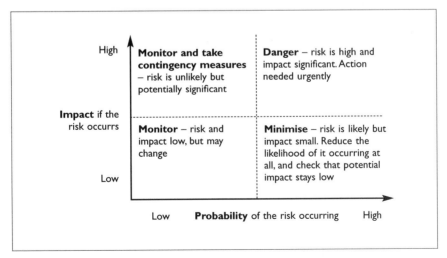

Figure 1.2 Managing the impact of risk

Prevailing logic says that having assessed each risk, appropriate strategies and priorities can then be established. So, that's sorted that then? If you have been following the arguments so far: perhaps not.

The first problem is that it is extremely difficult to *predict the impact* of a particular risk. Even if we could quantify any one of these categories, they do not reflect how the world works. There are not people risks, technical risks and so forth. There are just risks. Crucially, it is the interplay between these different categories that will determine the total impact. We are dealing here with the world of complexity in which things are not straightforward and causation is rarely if ever linear – certainly for the things that matter. Mathematicians from the end of the nineteenth century found that incredible complexity can quickly arise from the interplay of as little as three different independent bodies. Tackling risk like a 'laundry list' would almost certainly condemn you to some nasty surprises.

Complexity theory is beyond the scope of this book, but for anyone dealing with risk it is an essential area of understanding.[2] Not least because it helps us to understand that the world is not a predictable place with pockets of uncertainty but rather the reverse: essentially uncertain with small pockets of predictability.

This takes us to the second problem in which the effects of complexity apply. How much can we know about the *probability* of a particular event actually occurring? How confident can we be in probability at all?

The real problem here is measurement. It turns out to be difficult to measure the likelihood of something happening in the real world. Questions like 'do seat belts make it safer to drive or reduce injuries from road accidents?' turn out to be difficult to answer. Wearing a seat belt may well encourage us to drive faster as we feel more confident. Perhaps we could test this by looking at changes in the number of deaths on the road. But that would be confounded by the increase in motorists, power of vehicles, urbanisation of the countryside, even the introduction of other regulations such as drink-driving laws. The interplay of all of these factors makes accurately answering even a simple question like this almost impossible, and the conclusions drawn are based upon one perspective.

Furthermore, there is so much that we just plain do not know. Consider this statement from the National Research Council in the USA:

> The primary problem with risk assessment is that the information upon which decisions must be based is usually inadequate. Because the decision cannot wait, the gaps in information must be bridged by inference and belief, and these cannot be evaluated in the same way as facts.[3]

According to Adams, this situation is now more difficult. As scientists, technologists and traders identify and create new and more complex insights and products, we cannot keep up with the interactions and implications that result.

There is another factor that compounds the difficulties we have in assessing the probability of an event, one that is highlighted by the financial trader and mathematician Nassim Nicholas Taleb in his book *Fooled by Randomness*.[4] He argues that we have a disconcerting need to see patterns in unrelated events and make conclusions about what is going to happen next based upon rather shaky and flawed assumptions. People who do this are often applauded when things go well and derided when they don't, yet the results of either outcome may not be based upon any particular superior capability or knowledge. Taleb highlights the old problem of induction: you cannot draw a general law from a series of events, for there is always the possibility that the next event can disprove the theory. He argues that:

> At any point in time, a large section of businessmen with outstanding track records will be no better than randomly thrown darts. More curiously and owing to a peculiar bias, cases will abound of the least-skilled businessmen being the richest. However, they will fail to make an allowance for the role of luck in their performance!

To return to the point made earlier, risk-taking is more a matter of judgement than calculation; because of this, we cannot take out the perspective and perception of the potential risk taker. This introduces us to the central notion that risk is essentially subjective and audacity is therefore a particular human response to it.

Finally, Adams gives a poignant and powerful example of all of these issues. Worried parents live in houses that face a busy road. All day long, enormous trucks thunder up and down the road. The parents live in fear of their children running out onto the road or, perhaps even worse, a truck crashing through into where they play. They complain to the Department of Transport about the road. However, the number of deaths or serious accidents per kilometre constitutes the definition of a dangerous road. So, the road is not dangerous, according to the authorities. It continues to appear lethal to the parents who keep their children shut inside, thus ensuring that the authorities are right. The authorities' calculation and logic may be right, but their judgement is flawed because they do not fully understand the facts, in this case, the parents' response.

It is not our intention here to criticise risk management, and it may be that in some situations specific techniques have value. However, given that we cannot really know the odds or the full consequences as well as we would like, we are left with the challenge of understanding the psychological basis upon which we judge uncertainty and behave.

An unreasonable art

In the beginning there was no risk management. The gods decided in their capricious way how events unfolded, and man's job was to put up with it.

Later, mathematicians started using measurement as a way of taming uncertainty. In Peter Bernstein's book *Against the Gods*[5] he notes how the laws of probability grew up largely through analysis of games of chance, which in turn turned into the science of forecasting. He communicates the excitement of the breakthroughs of mathematicians like Pascal, who first came close to providing a theory of decision-making and who provided a mathematical basis for quantifiably anticipating future events.

The idea that decisions about risk are based upon the probability of an event occurring is powerfully implicit in the way we view uncertainty, often with the assumption that we prefer less risk rather than more. For example, it is generally held that most of us prefer comfort and safety to risk-taking. This belief has led to the widely held assumption that most of us are very cautious when it comes to uncertainty; furthermore, that risk-taking is for a psychologically different few. We will see that this is simply not true: all of us, on occasions, will seek the riskier alternative.

An important concept was added to the idea of probability, namely the concept of utility. Bernoulli in the eighteenth century was one of the first mathematicians to recognise that risk was also about the value of the risk to a particular person. His view was that this was essentially a rational process based upon the starting position of the risk taker. For example, if you were already wealthy, a small gain from a probable outcome would have less value for you. This notion is so implicit in much of our thinking today that we forget it was a breakthrough idea.

Although Bernoulli added the concept of subjectivity to our notions of risk-taking he essentially saw that the risk taker would act reasonably, based upon his or her circumstances. This view is shared by many of those who try to manage risk. The danger is that we end up with a blind faith in reason – that in all risk-taking we are essentially weighing up odds and benefits, attempting to manage an uncertain situation with a predisposition to take the most rational decision.

We have already shown that this is very problematic – with real life problems, we can rarely be sure of the odds or the impact of the event. However, even when we are sure this implied rationality is not as evident as might be assumed.

Some of the most powerful psychological research on risk is the work of Kahneman and Tversky. In a series of clever experiments involving decisions where the odds were clear and the benefits stated, they made a number of interesting discoveries:

- Emotion often destroys the self-control essential to rational decision-making.
- There are cognitive limits inhibiting our understanding of what we are dealing with, even in situations of moderate complexity.
- We display risk aversion in one setting when we are offered a choice, and risk seeking when we are offered the same choice in another setting.
- We pay excessive attention to low-probability events accompanied by high drama and overlook events that happen in a routine and low-key fashion.

Essentially, we are all inconsistent.

Many of these studies were based upon problems and games with a limited number of variables. Even so, as we have seen, individuals' decisions and actions are often counter to rationality. Kahneman and Tversky call this the 'failure of invariance'. If we prefer A to B, and B to C, then one could assume that rationally such a person would prefer A to C, and this is often not the case.

A common example of this is that investors are quite willing to take a profit on their investments but surprisingly unwilling to cut a loss. They cling on despite the evidence that things are getting worse. Kahneman and Tversky have called this 'loss aversion', claiming that losses have a bigger impact upon our attitudes to risk than gains – it may be that we take bigger risks to avoid a loss. For example, when they offered people a choice between taking the risk of an 80% chance of losing $4,000 and a 20% chance of breaking even, against a certainty of losing $3,000, 92% opted for the gamble. Yet if the mirror of the experiment is run, with the certainty of winning $3,000 versus an 80% chance of winning $4,000 versus 20% chance of winning nothing, 80% chose the certainty option of $3,000.[6]

This may seem very human but it is not rational.

A practical example of loss aversion with devastating consequences for many people was the action of a rogue trader at Barings Bank, Nick Leeson. He simply could not accept even a relatively normal loss in derivatives trading and so kept investing, fraudulently, to try and regain his mounting losses. By the time he was exposed, the bank had debts of hundreds of millions of pounds from this one trader.

Tversky and Kahneman went on to suggest that individuals make sense of the world by organising and interpreting events in terms of cause and effect reasoning.[7] The assumption of causality is one of the most fundamental structural features the human mind imposes on reality in order to make sense of it. We are predisposed to causal reasoning: a causal, methodical approach feels natural. Several researchers have established that people exhibit a high propensity to engage in causal reasoning when faced with important, unusual or surprising events.[8] These events create uncertainty that triggers the search for a causal agent, in the hope that by finding the causal agent control over the situation is re-established.[9]

Travelling the road to audacity

We can now draw several important conclusions:

- Real life situations make defining the odds difficult.
- Understanding the impact of risk is problematic at best.
- Risk-taking is a matter of subjective judgement, not calculation.
- The 'judge' is itself a factor in the level of risk.
- Judgement is not always rational. It is often emotional and inconsistent.

Faced with the sheer uncertainty of the world and our inability to rationally, cognitively cope with even moderate complexity, should we shrink back into helplessness? How can we move forward without certainty? How can we remain open to chance and surprise? How is it possible not to assume that because odds are unknown they must be insurmountable? How can we engage ourselves more fully in the exploration of a new terrain of opportunity? In truth, we have no choice. In organisations, which on average last much less than a human lifetime, we find that usually there is a failure to deal with uncertainty. Moreover, individually, not facing up to this challenge is to deny something about ourselves – the risk seeker in all of us.

It is for these reasons that we must embark upon the road to audacity.

In this book, our companions on this journey are not only businessmen in corporations but a whole array of people from all walks of life, from business to sports, from exploration to climbing, from politics to bullfighting.

Notes

1　Adams, J. (1995) *Risk*, Routledge, London
2　For further information about this topic, see Waldrop, Mitchell (1994) *Complexity*, Penguin, London
3　National Research Council (1983, reprinted 1992) *Risk Assessment in the Federal Government: Managing the Process*, National Academy Press, Washington DC
4　Taleb, N.N. (2001) *Fooled by Randomness – The Hidden Role of Chance in the Markets and in Life*, Texere, New York
5　Bernstein, P.L. (1998) *Against the Gods – The Remarkable Story of Risk*, Wiley, New York
6　Kahneman, D. and Tversky, A. (1979) Prospect Theory: An Analysis of Decision Under Risk, *Econometrica* **47**(2)
7　Tversky, A. and Kahneman, D. (1982) Causal Schemas in Judgements Under Uncertainty, in Kahneman, D., Slovic, P. and Tversky, A. (eds), *Judgement Under Uncertainty: Heuristics and Biases*, Cambridge University Press, Cambridge
8　See, for example, Kelly, G.A. (1994) *The Psychology of Personal Constructs*, 2nd edn, Routledge, London
9　Weiner, B. (1985) Spontaneous Causal Thinking, *Psychological Bulletin*, **97**: 74–84

CHAPTER TWO

Why? The Audacity Factor

Why be audacious?

A bullfighter is now judged and paid much more on his ability to pass the bull quietly, slowly, and closely with the cape than on his ability as a swordsman. (It) has become a moment of truth... The danger is so real, so controlled, and so selected by the man, and so apparent, and the slightest tricking or simulating of danger shows so clearly... The matadors rival each other in invention and in seeing with what purity of line, how slowly, and how closely they can make the horns of the bull pass their waists, keeping him dominated and slowing the speed of his rush with the sweep of the cape controlled by their wrists; the whole hot bulk of the bull passing the man who looks down calmly where the horns almost touch and sometimes do touch, his thighs while the bull's shoulders touch his chest, with no move of defence against the animal, and no move of defence against the death that goes by in the horns except the slow movement of his arms and his judgement of distance. (Ernest Hemingway, *Death in the Afternoon*[1])

Why?

Towards the end of the 1960s, as Mankind closed in on its goal of voyaging to the moon, nine men set out in small boats to race each other around the watery earth alone and without stopping. It had never been done before. Nobody knew if it could be... when they sailed, heading for the world's stormiest seas in a motley array of new and old boats, they vanished over the horizon into a true unknown. They failed and succeeded on the grandest scale. Only one of the nine crossed the finish line... For the others, the rewards were a rich mixture of failure, ignominy, madness and death. (Peter Nicholls, *A Voyage for Madmen*[2])

Why?

At 27 years old my father, with a wife and a young son, left the security of an established firm and reasonable salary on the promise of one piece of work, to set up on his own; within a few days of starting the promise of work evaporated.

Why? What is it that lies behind these behaviours that deliberately confront uncertainty and the unknown and raise the risk of failure, humiliation or even – in some cases – death? It is a timeless question. Why take the harder road? Why climb to the summit? Why leave the security of a well-paid job?

Why do we sometimes feel driven to turn dreams into reality?

The answers often come in the form of a helpless inarticulate mumble: 'Because of the buzz', 'To see if I could', or in the eloquent non-answer from mountaineer George Mallory, 'Because it's there'.

Understanding *why* is a fundamental challenge on the road to audacity. *Why?* is one question that must be addressed if we want to build lives and organisations that respond positively to uncertainty.

At a superficial level, the answer will often be varied and easy. In each case, there will a list of things to be gained such as fame, money, a new job or perhaps a new market. While this may expand our understanding of what may be achieved through audacity, it does not really explain why one person or group is audacious and another is not, nor at a more fundamental level what audacity actually is. Understanding more about the personal and private nature of the impulse towards audacity is an opportunity for liberation, to break free from tired ways of doing things, threadbare assumptions and the clinging, desperate need to look to someone else for our salvation.

The search for excitement

As we highlighted in the previous chapter, human beings seem drawn towards uncertainty on occasions. *Homo aleatorius*, risk seeker and 'dice man', lurks in all of us. We all seem in some way to want to seek out the unknown, turning deliberately towards uncertainty and doubt. The alternative seems unbearable.

Can we imagine a life of total uncertainty? A life at home or work where everything was totally predictable? Where each hour followed its carefully ordered and formulated path? A life in which every moment was inevitable?

However, we are not all the same in our search for excitement. We differ, but only in where we choose to confront uncertainty and the level that we find acceptable. For some, acceptable uncertainty is a round of bridge; for others it is betting the house on a hand of poker. Others find acceptable uncertainty when they are eyeball to eyeball with disaster on an ice wall above the clouds. Some people face up to a tricky putt on the seventeenth. In business, it can be Michael Dell choosing to rewrite the rules of the global computer business, or the person who gives up a well-paid job for a life less certain as a chef.

Whatever uncertainty we face and however we face it, to do so successfully can be immensely satisfying. More than that, excitement – even exhilaration – is our emotional reward for risk-taking.

Does that mean audacity is merely synonymous with a greater propensity to seek excitement? No. While we must account for the fact one person will find a particular risk exciting while another terrifying, this in itself is not enough. To construe audacity in this way would be a rather thin, pallid explanation. In the book *The Ulysses Factor*, J.R.L. Anderson wrote:

> Some force other than mere adventure must be looked for to discover what prompts a man not only to feel that it would be nice to know what is on the far side of the hills, but to contract a fever of desire to know, and then an absolute determination to find out.[3]

One of the crucial insights in discovering more about audacity is that within uncertainty and risk lies the potential for individuals to derive extraordinary reward. For those able to access this, life becomes deeper, richer and more meaningful.

The puzzle of why

In the course of preparing for this work one of the people interviewed was Phillip Whitehead, an acclaimed documentary film-maker with nearly forty years' distinguished service in public life, first as UK Member of Parliament then as a Member of the European Parliament. I asked whom he would rank, among all the distinguished people he had worked with or made films about, as the most audacious public figure he had met. Without hesitation, he highlighted Robert Kennedy, the assassinated US politician and brother of President John Kennedy. His reasons were illuminating, straight away capturing, unbidden, a sense of the wilfulness that lies within audacity:

> Given his name and the capital accrual that comes from the martyred brother, and all the riches of his family, he could have been just a team player and

struck a bargain that he got a big cabinet position or something and then became the acknowledged successor (to Lyndon Johnson). But he broke with that, to the rage of many people. He was a high-risk player.

In pursuing nomination as a presidential candidate, he thought long and hard and started re-educating himself. Millionaire's son though he was, he visited and listened to poor people. He met the leaders of the famous workers' strike in California, he went south and met not just leaders of the Southern Baptist Church and Martin Luther King, but also people who were much more radical. These people expressed a view that unless you had a total turnaround in addressing all these fundamental discontents there would be an immense problem. I watched him and was emotionally moved when, for example, in front of a black audience he suddenly got up and read out the Langston Hughes poem about the dilemma of the American Black people: 'What happens to a dream deferred? Does it dry up like a raisin in the sun? Does it fester like a sore and run? Or does it explode?'

I mean he saw how close the explosion was, and I think that it radicalised him and made him reach for the presidency. I remember he addressed a rally in Georgia on the day that Martin Luther King was murdered. He had to stand on a platform immediately in front of an audience of angry, wounded blacks who had seen their leader slaughtered that day by a white man. He stood there – a rich, white man – and made this extraordinary speech as the brother of someone who had also been killed by a white man, and he brought them round! I saw at that moment, unlikely as it seemed, that this guy could really have done it, raising passions to heal divisions. Someone who, like Martin Luther King, spoke every day looking down the barrel of a gun, emerging from the most unlikely of backgrounds to be a force for good. (From an interview with Phillip Whitehead)

It would be outrageous to trivialise the behaviour of such people as merely motivated by excitement-seeking.

The same seems to be true in other walks of life. In business, Richard Branson, founder of the Virgin Group, is a man who, having built a media empire, took the huge risk of launching the airline Virgin Atlantic within four months of first discussing the idea. He also founded and supports the Student Advisory Centre and is an employer who can claim, with some justification, to put his employees first. To many, Branson is motivationally an enigma. To some, he is a self-serving publicist whose every action is aimed at furthering his own needs; to others, he is a role model of what a responsible, modern businessman should be like. In one survey, he was Britain's preferred choice as Prime Minister! The only thing that people seem to agree on is that he is a supremely audacious businessman. Undoubtedly bold, what drives him can seem enigmatic and contradictory.

The previous chapter explored the multifaceted way we use the idea of audacity in real life. This is echoed wherever we start to examine the motives and behaviours of those we call audacious. The nine lone sailors in Peter Nicholls's *A Voyage for Madmen*, attempting to make the first non-stop solo circumnavigation of the world,

> sailed for reasons more complex than even they knew. Each decided to make his voyage independent of the others; the race between them was born only of the coincidence of their timing... Their preparations and their boats were as varied as their personalities and the contrasts were startling.

The puzzle that makes audacity so fascinating is the puzzle of *why*. What is it about certain people that encourages or enables them to behave on occasions in a way that can seem pointless or even self-destructive?

Is there some unique quality to Robert Kennedy, Richard Branson, circumnavigators and others of this world who are manifestly audacious? Are some individuals born audacious, or is it something that we as individuals and collectively in organisations can develop?

Born audacious?

People have felt tempted to say that audacious people are in some ways different from the rest of us. Legend and writers have often remarked on the image of the heroic loner, taking on the world and prepared to sacrifice everything in pursuit of some dream. To deliberately impoverish themselves, risk death and humiliation, scorn fame and fortune. Surely such people are not like us? Do they deal with the world in the same way or face the same challenges, issues and fears? J.R.L. Anderson wrote in *The Ulysses Factor* about such people possessing a genetic factor that exists in all of us but is suppressed in most. It is seen as a form of special adaptation, which prompts a few individuals to exploits that, however purposeless they may seem in themselves, are of value to the survival of the race.

In other words, such people have an adaptive role to play in the evolution of various societies – their success and impact promoted by specific environmental conditions so that they play a determining role in the destiny of a social or cultural group. Examples of such people include the Phoenicians *c.*10th century BC, Greek society in the 8th century BC, Persian and Arab societies in the 6th century. More recent examples include Scandinavian peoples from the 8th to the 11th centuries, the Spanish and Portuguese in the 14th and 15th centuries, the British in the

16th century and the British (again) and the French in the 18th and 19th centuries. Anderson goes further than this, defining the characteristics of people who have inherited this genetic factor and seeing their archetype as the legendary hero Ulysses (hence the Ulysses factor). These characteristics include courage, selfishness, practical competence, physical strength, powerful imagination, ability to lead, self-discipline, endurance, self-sufficiency, cunning, unscrupulousness and a strong sexual attraction. Quite a list, and quite a dangerous one to put in a recruitment advertisement! There are echoes within it of our discussions earlier on the notion of audacity, and certainly the story of Ulysses reflects the simile that audacity is like a journey. Putting aside for a while the question of how true the list is, the question is whether these are characteristics that one may reasonably be said to be born with.

As we have already noted (and without entering a circular debate about nature versus nurture), people differ in the amount of uncertainty that they feel able to deal with, and it is possibly the case that there is a significant genetic component to this. It is certainly the case that at a primitive level we respond emotionally to acts and people that we view as being audacious. (As a child, I can easily remember the excitement and national acclamation that arose as Francis Chichester, a bespectacled, balding, scrawny guy of 65, returned to England, having sailed around the world, stopping only once in Australia. The whole country became obsessed with the story.)

However, before we helplessly consign audacity to the genetically blessed, we should investigate the extent to which people can be said to become more or less audacious. Through our work with many organisations, talking in depth to people who have been responsible for behaviours deemed by others to be audacious, through looking at the research, some of which is highlighted below, we have reached the inevitable conclusion that there is a developmental aspect to audacity.

The problem with instinct theories is that they rather let you off the hook in terms of needing to develop, encourage or maintain audacity – for you either have it or you don't. These theories do not account for the person who after a lifetime of funk suddenly amazes everyone by taking on an Everest of a challenge. Or the gung-ho Major who falters. Or the fact there are some arenas of action in which we feel audacious and others in which to take any sort of risk would reduce us to a gibbering wreck. From an organisational point of view, the implication is that those organisations wanting to act more audaciously in the face of uncertainty are left with one option. To buy enough audacious people to meet the challenge of change, while simultaneously encouraging other mere mortals to follow as best they can.

It is a fundamental assumption of this book that individually and as organisations we can all become more audacious, and in fact more successfully audacious. To achieve this we face three essential challenges:

- To understand systematically how we deal with the world.
- To understand where audacity fits within this.
- To start down the road to audacity.

We start with the first challenge: understanding how we deal with the world.

The promise of inconsistency

Audacity is a special form of human experience, but it does sit within the general scope of what it is to be human. What we need is a framework in which to understand human behaviour in all its facets, one that offers a way of understanding the complexity of audacity that we have already started to highlight.

A contemporary theory of the human experience that is elegant and goes a long way to helping our understanding is called *reversal theory*. This psychological theory offers compelling insights into how individuals are motivated, and in what ways their motivation can express itself in audacious behaviour. It helps us understand more about the mindset of the thrusting tycoons, the bullfighters, the political dynasties and the circumnavigators, to uncover the rich mystery of audacity – one that moves it far beyond the calculation of odds and the objective analysis of statistics or even the simple search for a high, to the essence of what it is to be human.

Dr Michael Apter and Dr Ken Smith, working in the UK in the late 1970s, originally formulated reversal theory. Since then, it has been taken up by over fifty universities worldwide, and many hundreds of research papers have been published about the insights it offers in the fields of health and sports psychology, physiological psychology, humour and art as well as more general research. It has been especially fruitful in looking at a wide variety of risk-taking behaviour and describing the circumstances in which people will undertake 'risky' behaviour.

More recently, I have been exploring the application of reversal theory to the world of work along with Mike Apter. What follows is an outline of the theory itself, and how it helps to explain the 'why' of audacity.

At the heart of reversal theory is a fundamental insight into human nature that how we behave depends upon how we motivationally interpret the world at a given moment and that:

> We are not always the same: we are inconsistent, we develop and we change, We are different people at different times, even under the same circumstances. What we see as important one moment can seem unimportant the next, and although there may be patterns to this we would not over-rely upon them. Each of us inhabit eight ways of being, combinations of which determine how we interact with a situation.[4]

These eight ways of being will be discussed more fully in the next chapter, but for the moment it is enough to highlight that they describe eight different motivational states arranged in opposite pairs. Our experience is shaped by the patterns in which we switch (or reverse) between pairs of opposite motivational states, and the ways in which different pairs become more or less important. At the heart of each state is a value (such as rebellious or conforming, serious or playful) that expresses itself in what we feel is important at a given moment, the emotions we experience and, in a more indirect way, the behaviours we pursue.

It is a bit like switching lenses on a given situation. One colour lens may make things look dark and gloomy, and we would want to avoid it, whereas another appears bright and fun, enticing us to stay. Another example is the famous drawing of the old lady or young girl. Depending upon what you see may well lead you to offer a cup of tea or an invitation to dance.

Our lives are made up of these switches and changes. Who we are is not fixed, and inconsistency is our birthright. Unfortunately, it is not a right we give easily to others. We demand, no doubt for good reasons, that people are consistent. We feel uncomfortable if they are not and we doubt their intentions.

For all I know, the most benevolent of business leaders may sometimes be a self-oriented manipulator. But then again, this does not mean that he is not driven on other occasions to be powerfully committed to help others in the most genuine way. Reversal theory does not propose that personality is some variable mid-point between these two extremes, but rather that we can be fully and vigorously motivated either way on separate occasions. Also, although the specifics of the situation can determine how we are motivated, they do not necessarily do so. Frustration or even just being in a particular state for a length of time can lead us to change or to 'reverse' into another state (hence the name of the theory), which causes us to reinterpret that situation and behave quite differently.

Put another way, what seems to be excitingly audacious in the evening can seem foolhardy and pointless the next morning – or even the second after conceiving it.

Our motivation is elusive and chameleon-like: the trivial can suddenly seem transcendent, the great victory may feel worthless. The rugged path one day beckons and the next is abandoned to more gentle, friendlier pursuits. Contestants become friends. Our lives are the pattern of these changes. Sometimes these changes are slow: in some situations what we see as critical can call us forward for years on end; sometimes the changes can happen within seconds.

Our inconsistency means that a simple single reward will rarely keep us going. While our behaviour generally matures and we manage to establish some coherence in our lives, underneath is either a shifting pattern of emotions, or frustration as the narrowness of life forces us to forget what we want. To be fulfilled, we need to keep all eight of us happy! All eight of our motivational states need to be accessed for fulfilment. Lifestyles and work environments do not typically make this easy, and somewhere along the way we may lose sight of how to live successfully in all of these eight states.

What uncertainty offers

Uncertainty guarantees nothing, but it often provides a promise of hidden rewards. As we highlighted in the last chapter, organisations find that economic value can be found by exploiting scarcity, and this invariably involves risk. In creating a new venture, we will potentially gain much more than a new set of business results. On a personal level, we don't know exactly what we will get out of climbing to the summit, but we can be sure it will be different from what we expect.

The special thing about being audacious is that it is a means of harnessing uncertainty, ambiguity or even threat in a way that allows us to contribute and gain reward in almost uniquely rich and powerful ways. The destination and the journey, the map and exploration, the struggle for power and the close-knit band, the loner and the sacrifice for others, all contain the potential for reward in different states, as we shall see.

Audacity allows us to be essentially contradictory, different things at different times and to take full account of our complexity. Audacity is an approach to uncertainty that allows the bullfighter to be exhilarated, proud, to be part of an elite group, to achieve wealth and fame, to stand apart through greater courage, skill and approach. Bullfighters are realising a dream – no one becomes a bullfighter without wanting it – and this shows why striving to be audacious is worthwhile: because it is fulfilling.

Audacity enables the committed politician to be radical and conservative (isn't every politician except for an absolute anarchist at some level a map follower?), to inflate a mighty ego, to be passionately committed to helping others.

Audacity enables the entrepreneur to do something different and revel in the freedom of it, to pursue personal interests with passion and excitement, to potentially gain wealth and status.

In considering our approach to an uncertain world, it is this 'audacity factor' we need to capture. The potential lies within us all, for a mindset that coolly and completely faces up to the rewards and opportunities of uncertainty.

The first stop on the road to audacity is the eight states, the mechanisms by which we change and the implications of this for organisations and for us as individuals.

Notes

1 Hemingway, E. (1996) *Death in The Afternoon*, Touchstone, New York
2 Nicholls, P.A. (2001) *A Voyage for Madmen*, Profile Books, London
3 Anderson, J.R.L. (1970) *The Ulysses Factor*, Hodder & Stoughton, London
4 Apter, M. *Apter Motivational Style Profile Consultant Guide*, Apter International, Loughborough, p. 6

CHAPTER THREE

The Eight Ways of Being

Imagine this. You are on 'The Vortex of Certain Death', the latest fun ride at a major amusement park. Firmly strapped into your seat alongside one hundred other terrified, screaming people, you are being slowly pulled up to a great height. At the apex of your ascent you will then be turned rapidly through 720 degrees. Before you can orient yourself you then plummet through an enormous wall of fire. Hopefully emerging from the other side, you find yourself rushing at a seemingly fantastic speed towards what appears to be a formidable rock wall. As you bellow out an incoherent and terror-struck request for someone to stop the ride immediately, the ride itself executes another dizzyingly fast manoeuvre, misses the wall and comes to rest in a large, and until that point unseen, trough of water.

Unsteadily, you stagger away with an inane grin on your face. Someone asks you whether you enjoyed it. 'Absolutely brilliant!' you exclaim, 'What a rush.' You probably don't explain you have just spent twenty seconds of your life, plus 55 minutes before as you queued for the ride, alternating between terror and exhilaration with increasing regularity.

It was in an effort to understand why at least some of us would want to undertake such an apparently pointless act, and how we typically respond to it, that Mike Apter and his colleagues developed from the late 1970s a dynamic account of human experience. This approach, known as reversal theory, was radically at odds with more static accounts of human motivation. The outcome was a general theory of how we behave and experience things, derived from an analysis of motivation in many different cultures, settings and organisations. It has been and continues to be internationally researched, and is now backed by an impressive body of evidence. It has demonstrated its value in many areas including child guidance, sports psychology, health and stress management, as well as management and leadership. The theory provides a comprehensive account of what it is really like to be human and offers powerful insights into how we can build personal lives and organisations that are more adventurous. Although chapters on theory tend to be skimmed or skipped, we do recommend that this one is read; the rest of the book does depend upon grasping the essential features of the theory and the implications that can be drawn from them.

Consistently inconsistent: how we deal with arousal

The bedrock understanding of the theory comes from insights and discoveries about the inconsistent way in which we deal with arousal. Typically, psychologists have tended to view whether we experience arousal (defined as a physiological response to stimulation from the environment such as danger, sexual opportunity, perceived risk and so forth) as pleasant or not as depending upon the degree of arousal. This was classically described by Canadian neurologist Donald Hebb (see Figure 3.1) in terms of an optimal arousal curve.[1] It suggests that we experience increasing arousal as increasingly pleasurable until some optimum point is reached, after which arousal is experienced as increasingly unpleasant, leading eventually to high levels of anxiety.

This idea of optimal arousal has achieved a level of orthodoxy in our understanding of how we deal with uncertainty and risk. It can be characterised as 'give me a high level of arousal, but not too high'.

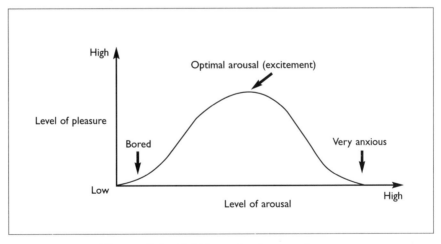

Figure 3.1 Hebb's optimal arousal curve

Source: Reproduced from Apter, M.J. (1989) *Reversal Theory: Motivation, Emotion and Personality*, Routledge, London

Mike Apter increasingly came to see something rather peculiar in this model and proposition. At first intuitively, and then through a series of experiments he challenged this orthodoxy, making some interesting observations:

- I don't seem to pass through maximum pleasure (optimum arousal) on my way to the dentist – I seem to move straight to maximum anxiety.
- Wild sex is about as arousing as it gets and yet in only a few cases does it result in massive anxiety. (Using the Hebb formulation, I guess you would end up with the rather traditional British perspective on love-making – yes please, but not too much.)
- Soldiers charging to near certain death often report feeling excited or even exhilarated.

Mike Apter proposed that two *different* arousal curves are available to us and that we can interpret arousal in two different ways, as shown in Figure 3.2. On one curve, high arousal is seen as exciting and low arousal as boring, on the other curve we move from pleasant relaxation to high anxiety. The difference depends upon how we perceive a particular situation and what we feel is important at any moment. In one instance, the 'arousal-seeking' case, Apter suggests that we are viewing a situation very much from the point of view of its present value here and now. We are looking at it in terms of its intrinsic potential to offer through excitement or absorbing interest immediate reward. In the second 'arousal-avoiding'

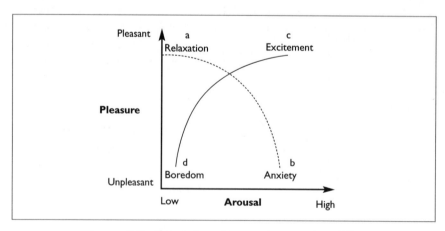

Figure 3.2 Arousal-seeking and arousal-avoiding

Source: Reproduced from Apter, M.J. (1989) *Reversal Theory: Motivation, Emotion and Personality*, Routledge, London

case, we are viewing the situation very much from its potential consequences, including its potential to harm or reward us or to achieve some other goal located in the future.

This analysis will explore the first two of the eight ways of being analysed more fully below, but straight away it is important to make a key point: in any situation we do not often stay on one curve. Importantly, we can switch or reverse between these two curves at any moment, either because some aspect of the situation changes or because we become frustrated.

To give a practical example, imagine sailing home on an evening tide after a great day and with a friendly breeze, looking forward to a safe berth and a drink at the pub. Life is glorious. Then quite suddenly the sky darkens, the wind freshens and changes direction. The entrance to the harbour all of a sudden looks very difficult and the rocks either side, now increasingly lashed by wave and wind, appear very threatening. Your mood changes to one of concern and trepidation.

Or, imagine really enjoying working on a particular piece of work. You find it really interesting and are enjoying discovering new and unexpected things as you work on it. But then you get stuck and start to lose interest in the whole enterprise. You would really like to put it down and do something else but you are committed to a deadline and find yourself anxious about completing it on time, so you press on.

This emotional switching or reversals is not just one-way, and we can experience all aspects of both curves within a given situation.

An example of this can be shown with another scenario from work. You are responsible for introducing an important new process into the manufacturing plant. It requires millions of dollars of investment from your company. You are coming up to switch-over day and things have gone well. You are at point (a) (see Figure 3.2). However, with a few hours to go a major technical problem arises. You curse yourself for not seeing sooner the potential for this happening. Rapidly you find yourself at point (b) and very worried. You call a crisis meeting. A recovery plan is drawn up and everyone gets very busy. For a while, things still seem very uncertain, but deeply immersed in the action you find yourself feeling more and more in control and enjoying the challenge of saving the day. You are at point (c). Sometimes a new bit of information arises and the fears return, switching you momentarily back to (b). However, as the deadline approaches you are revelling in the exhilaration of months of struggle coming to fruition. Switch-over occurs and everything goes better than expected. The mood among the team is almost like a party. Later you sit back quietly on your own, feeling relaxed and satisfied (a) at a job well done. After a few days, you might even begin to miss the excitement and feel a little bored, reaching point (d).

Walters, Apter and Svebak obtained early scientific evidence of these reversals.[2] Using changes in colour preference (previously established as relating to preferred levels of arousal), the study demonstrated that office workers within the course of a normal working day regularly fluctuated between choosing as preference short-wave arousal-reducing colours such as blue, violet and indigo, and long-wave arousing colours such as red, orange and yellow. Other sampling techniques produced similar results. The impact of these and other studies provides powerful evidence suggesting the paradoxical notion of man as both risk taker and risk avoider.

The insights of reversal theory are important. They show not just that individuals differ between themselves (meaning that some tend to be more often arousal-seeking than others), but also that the same individual seems to be able to experience either curve at different times, *even when the situation appears the same and no obvious frustration is experienced*. It is not, therefore, just situation changes and frustration that trigger this inconsistency and changeability: it appears to be an essential aspect of our programming as humans. In a series of experiments, Kathy Lafreniere and her colleagues[3] showed that given access to opportunities relating to both curves, participants would spontaneously switch between them. Apter has termed this phenomenon 'satiation'.

Satiation suggests that we as humans are inherently unstable, regardless of external circumstances. In short, we are wired-up excitement seekers – sometimes.

Experiencing the world

Having established the essentially inconsistent way in which we deal with arousal, Michael Apter and his colleagues have subsequently gone on to propose a framework for understanding how we react to the world and what motivates us. The eight ways of being that have already been discussed fall as four pairs of opposites, each pair addressing a different aspect (or using its technical term, domain) of our experience.[4] Successfully confronting uncertainty and risk involves us responding to all four aspects of experience in positive ways. The four domains of experience make up the building blocks out of which we construe our own personal reality (Figure 3.3).

Each of these domains of experience contains two different ways of orienting ourselves towards the world, the changing focus between these two determining which motivational state someone is in at a given time.

What does being in a motivational state mean?

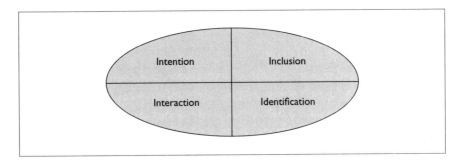

Figure 3.3 The four domains of experience

It is a way of seeing the world, and it determines what we will be motivated by and how we will respond to what is happening around us. It is not a particular mood or emotion but rather 'A higher order that represent a range of possible specific emotions, and a class of things, which come to the foreground of attention and can provide pleasure or pain.'[5]

The motivational states are like lenses of different colours and shapes through which we interpret and interact with the world. A different lens moves us from one range of emotions, values and motivators to another – hence another way of being. This concept becomes clearer as we examine each domain of experience in turn.

Intention: goals versus means

This aspect of experience deals with fundamentally *why* at any given moment we are doing something. Our experience of intention is always made up of both the goal itself and the means by which we pursue that goal. For example, a business wants to expand (goal) by purchasing a rival (means). A comedian wants to earn a living (goal) by making people laugh (means). An explorer wants to explore a new route across the desert (goal) by mapping out the unknown (means). Intentions can be noble or ignoble, grandiose or pathetic, but they will always need to involve a goal and a means.

There is nothing hugely insightful so far, but reversal theory does challenge a hidden assumption in this: that the means is always a servant of the goal. The insights of Apter and his colleagues suggest that the opposite can also be true: that the goal of a situation can be the servant of the means. This takes us back to an earlier discussion, the idea of the destination and the journey. Sometimes we travel because we need to get somewhere – the

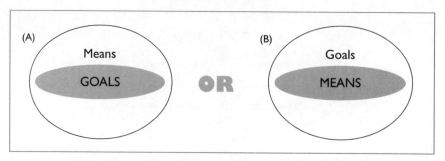

Figure 3.4 Goals and means in the intention domain

means being relatively unimportant. On other occasions the travel itself is what we seek, and a destination merely stops us going around in circles.

So, within the domain it is possible either to be focusing on the destination or the journey, the goal or the means. Gestalt psychology has talked about perception consisting of figure and ground, and this idea neatly summarises the argument here. Reversals switch figure to ground and ground to figure, as highlighted in Figure 3.4.

Depending upon which perception we have, we will value different things, experience different emotions and tend to engage in different behaviours. The goal/means configuration determines which motivational state we are in within a specific domain – in this case *intention*. When the goal is to the forefront of our experience (A), we are said to be in a *serious* state, and when the means dominates our experience (B), we are said to be in a *playful* state.

The serious and playful states relate directly to the discoveries regarding arousal-avoiding and arousal-seeking, and were the first to be specifically defined within reversal theory.

When we are in a serious state we particularly value achievement. This encourages us to see and react to the world in a particular way: certain things we will tend to ignore or not notice, while others will be very important to us. We are motivated to do those things that will ensure we achieve a particular goal. We will want to plan, minimise the risk that the goals won't be achieved, and remove anything that will distract us from our objectives. We will look at whatever we are immediately doing in terms of how it enables us to reach our objective. In this state, our focus is on the future, even if the future is only a few minutes away. When we become excited psychologically or physiologically through focus and effort, we tend to become anxious and concerned, for example, that we might not meet our goal.

We can be in a serious state both at work and at home. Out of work hours, we can be obsessive about achieving particular goals, feeling anxious when things are going badly and feeling deep satisfaction and fulfilment when we have achieved them. It is important to realise, therefore, that the serious state does not refer to something that is held to be important in any abstract sense, but only to a view that we have of a particular situation.

The same is true of the term playful, which can be mistakenly seen as relating to trivial situations. In fact, when we are in this state of mind we react to the world in a very different way. What matters in this state are questions such as: Am I enjoying this? Is it interesting? Is it fun? What motivates people in this state are activities and opportunities that are intrinsically interesting or exciting. In this state, when we become excited through focus, challenge and effort we tend to feel excited – and the greater the uncertainty the better. If you are unconvinced about how uncertainty can be beneficial and exciting and motivational, think for a moment what it would be like to play a game in which you knew every time that you would win without any difficulty. Would you not get bored? Surely, the uncertainty and challenge of playing a game is central to its point?

It is very easy to dismiss the value of the playful state as having no relevance to the world of work. In fact, managers in several organisations that we have worked with – including a major US global business and a slightly smaller British one – have rejected the word and its associations. 'There should be no playfulness in our organisation', they grimly assert. 'What we require is a workforce totally focused on tight goals!' Is it any wonder that modern organisations are stricken with anxiety, often forced to invest in new and imaginative ways of attracting, retaining and motivating people, to counter the new and imaginative ways they have found of repelling, rejecting and demoralising people?

Such organisations fundamentally misunderstand the significance and richness of the playful state. In this motivational state, people tend to stay longer on a difficult task, work harder, and are usually more creative and innovative. Playfulness is at the heart of productivity and by implication profitability.

An inspiring example of the playful state is the case of Gary Flandro. During the mid-1960s Flandro was an undergraduate student on a work placement with NASA, the space agency. At that time, NASA was in the middle of the first Mariner missions to Mars as well as the Apollo programme, and Flandro was given the task of calculating the orbits of the outer planets. It was a task that his supervisors thought would be interesting for an undergraduate on a short placement, and it would keep him out of the way of the serious stuff that was happening at the agency, the Mars missions in particular. Flandro approached the task enthusiastically and imaginatively. He discovered that the four largest planets in the solar system would be on the same side of the Sun, in the same proximity, only once every 175 years. He then calculated that a mission to Jupiter and the outer planets (Saturn, Uranus and Neptune) would be possible because of the planets' proximity to each other, and the fact that the gravitational field of one planet could slingshot a probe onto another target at even greater speed. Flandro's discovery led to NASA launching the enormously successful Pioneer and Voyager space probes during the 1970s that dramatically increased our understanding of the solar system. Not bad for a playful undergraduate given a routine task to complete! (Impressive though this example is for Gary Flandro, it also seems impressive that NASA had the capacity to recognise the significance of his work at a time when it had other major projects in progress.)

Playfulness is therefore the arousal-seeking state in which we most enthusiastically face the unknown. Although the serious state has much to contribute to successful audacity, playfulness is at its core. The great English explorer, ethnologist, cartographer, photographer and author, Freya Stark, acknowledges this point:

> I must admit, for my own part I travelled single-mindedly for fun. I learnt my scanty Arabic for fun, and a little Persian – and then went for the same reason to look for the Assassin Castles and the Luristan bronzes… I know in my heart of hearts that it is a most excellent reason to do things merely because one likes the doing of them.[6]

Inclusion: fitting in versus falling out

Reversal theory proposes a similar construction for the second domain of experience I have called *inclusion*. Experience always takes place within a framework of rules, and sociologists spend much of their time trying to uncover these rules, which are rarely formal or explicit. These are rules that govern our experience and may include cultural norms and customs, rules of behaviour, codes of practice and assumptions about how the world works. They form a channel through which behaviour can be focused. They are essential to the operation of any organisation, project or initiative. Similarly, an adventurous activity also has rules covering issues such as safety, established routes to be followed, conventions among its participants, and so forth.

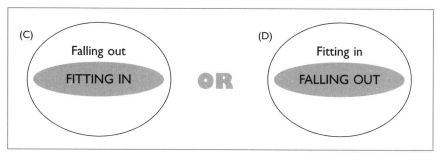

Figure 3.5 Fitting in and falling out in the inclusion domain

Rules in this way are like maps. They comfort us by helping us know what to do and where to go – in this case in our interactions with others. Crucially, following rules is a way of signalling that we belong. However, we can respond to rules and expectations as something constraining and inhibiting, something to be broken.

As before, we find within this aspect of experience two elements that can produce contrary motivational states (Figure 3.5).

This view exists because it seems psychologically that the possibility of each must exist for the other to be experienced successfully. There must be rules to follow if breaking them is to have any meaning. Similarly, it must be possible to conceive of breaking rules if to be following them is to have any meaning.

The absence of either can have important consequences for us psychologically. Asha Phillips, a child psychotherapist, in discussing the Everest-like challenge of parenting teenagers, has written:

> During adolescence, rules are often fought against, limits considered frustrating and at times even crippling. Does this mean that we should give them up? The need (not to) is two-fold. Firstly, the young adolescent needs parents to struggle against... He may argue with you as a way of finding out what he really thinks, he may reject your point of view in order to look for his own way. Secondly, of course, there are times when you need to say no firmly. Sometimes the child really wants you to restrict him; he is frightened or worried about something but does not want to lose face in front of others.[7]

Sociologists would also probably want to point out that organisationally, not giving enough attention to both of these elements would create deep organisational issues. To remove the possibility of falling out would, according to Marx and his followers, create the conditions for alienation in which organisational members feel they have no choice but to follow external, rigidly imposed rules. This in turn leads to feelings of worthlessness, powerlessness and denial of individuality.

The sociologist Durkheim[8] gave an equally depressing vision of a society or an organisation in which there were no rules. He described a condition of *anomie*, in which there were no established norms or expectations, leading to chaos, irresponsible goal-setting, disorientation and even self-destruction. *Anomie* motivates 'a search for social stability, security and certainty'.[9]

The state (C) in which fitting-in figures is termed the *conformist* state. When we are in this state we derive pleasure from meeting expectations, while organisationally contributing by making sure things happen in the way that they are supposed to. It is often at the heart of what makes us adaptable and willing to work effectively with others. Also, it often provides the source of an easy-going and relaxed view of life.

Our desire to fit in and be accepted is both an individual state and a social phenomenon – it is the glue that holds organisations and society together. It can be found in the shared beliefs we have about how things work, what we sometimes think of as common sense. For example, it is common sense in one organisation that you should get approval from a senior manager before embarking on a capital spending project. It is clearly common sense that customers will stay loyal if we offer better service at a lower price. It is common sense that you should make sure you have the best education possible. Our shared common sense is a reflection of our conformity.

The reverse of this is the *rebellious* state (D). Here, falling out is key, refusing to fit in, to do things the accepted, expected way. When combined with a serious state, frustration in this state is the source of anger. More mildly, when we are also in the playful state rebellion combines to lead us to be mischievous. Rebellion is all about freedom, challenging the status quo. We can see it constantly in audacious acts or behaviour. It is the source of the wilfulness we have already remarked upon. It is what made Robert Kennedy redefine himself politically, Churchill not to capitulate, Picasso to redefine what was expected in painting. As we shall see in later chapters, it is what made Graham Mackay at SABMiller think beyond the politics and constraints of South Africa, Tim Smit to conceive of The Eden Project, and Chris McHugo to renovate the Kasbah at the foot of Mount Toukbahl.

An organisation that inhibits individuals from being in the rebellious state, or individuals who do not express themselves within this state, should consider the following words from Alain De Botton:

It is not only the hostility of others that may prevent us from questioning the status quo. Our will to doubt can just as powerfully be sapped by an internal sense that societal conventions must have a sound basis, even if we are not sure exactly what this may be, because they have been adhered to by a great many people for a long time. It seems implausible that our society could be gravely mistaken in its beliefs and at the same time we would be alone in noticing the fact. We stifle our doubts and follow the flock because we cannot conceive ourselves as pioneers of hitherto, unknown, difficult truths.[10]

Interaction: transactions versus relationships

Interaction is the domain of experience that determines how we engage with people or things in the world. Together with the last domain of iden-tification, it encompasses the extremes of human nature, from the noblest self-sacrifice to the ruthless exploitation and even destruction of others. Within the domain of interaction we can focus either on the transaction or the relationship (Figure 3.6).

Transactions are about the 'deal'. When it is to the fore, we are concerned with who wins or loses, who is up or down. The motivational state that arises from this arrangement of the elements is termed *mastery* (E). In this state, our experiences are around power and control. It is about domination and competence (either for ourselves or others). Success in this state makes us feel proud, whereas failure results in a sense of humili-ation. Motivation in this state is at the heart of our restless desire to improve, whether it is for some greater purpose (serious) or as an end in itself (playful).

The pleasure we get from mastery thus stimulates learning. Moreover,

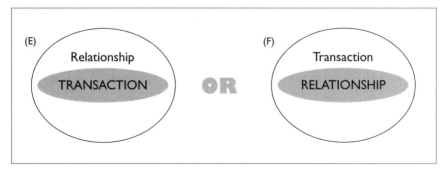

Figure 3.6 Transaction and relationship in the interaction domain

mastery provides the heartbeat for any sport. In the view of Michael Apter and John Kerr:

> Competitive sport is the very epitome of mastery play, being centred around the attempt to master various physical skills and to dominate and control the opposition. It is about contest, trial and confrontation. The very concept of beating or vanquishing an opponent in football or basketball or hockey expresses the mastery orientation, as indeed does the concept of defeat. But in a similar way, all those pursuits or sports which involve the individual pitting himself against the elements, as in mountaineering, cross-country skiing, surfing, hang-gliding and pot-holing… are manifestations of the mastery state. Again, there are games such as gambling and gaming in which the challenge comes from exposing oneself to risk with the chance of prevailing over the odds.[11]

However, mastery has dangers, particularly in extreme cases where the relationship element is poorly represented. In this state, we can easily start to see people as objects and treat them as such. Evils such as forms of personal violence are extreme examples where the mastery state enables individuals to interpret the world without the inhibition of a background consideration of relationships and issues such as feelings and an empathic acknowledgement of impact. (The often-reported feelings of remorse and self-loathing that succeed these acts are a good example of a reversal.)

In fact, we can also even treat ourselves as objects. In conversations we have had with climbers, explorers and the general collection of people who could be termed much-tougher-than-us, it was a recurring theme that they were prepared to abuse themselves to the point of considerable personal damage!

It could be reasonably argued that this is one of the hidden dangers of audacity.

The inversion of elements here provides the motivational state that is termed *sympathy* (F). In this state considerations of the relationship predominate. People are seen in terms of emotional beings rather than objects to be manipulated. We are motivated to consider others, to like and be liked.

We often have problems in discussing this state and its impact upon our lives. Its value in the world of business and its relevance to audacity are frequently underestimated, yet the ability to understand and work well with others is surely vital in any venture or adventure. The capacity to offer sympathy and affection is part of what defines us as people, and its absence massively inhibits trust, understanding and, ultimately, effective working.

It is easy to make assumptions about which of these states someone is in from their behaviour. In a study of health behaviour, O'Connell and

Brooks found that taking exercise, normally associated with the mastery state, can in fact be prompted by the sympathy state, a desire to nurture oneself.[12] This is an important insight from reversal theory and highlights the point that in thinking about any aspect of human performance we should consider carefully exactly what is going on.

Understanding the mastery and sympathy states can illuminate two quite different, divergent standpoints of behaviour that on the surface may seem very similar (an important insight of reversal theory). For example, consider a salesman who ruthlessly exploits his customers to get a sale, not really caring how the customer will feel later. Another salesman will focus more on the relationship he has with his customers, making sure that this is much more based upon friendship and trust. The former clearly operates mostly from a state of mastery whereas in the other sympathy is the dominant state. Sure, the second salesman may be clear that in the end this approach should benefit himself from a mastery (and self-orientation) point of view. However, there is a mutuality here that the purely transaction-based salesman is blind to.

It is tempting to hypothesise that one of the most profound aspects of Robert Kennedy's reinvention of himself (highlighted in the previous chapter) is that in a sympathy state he genuinely connected and cared about the people he tried to help. This came across as different from many politicians whose espoused concern for people is often read as self-serving and manipulative. Perhaps it is for this reason that an emotional connection to Kennedy's values still echoes down the years.

Audacity without the sympathy state would be a kind of mania, and would almost inevitably fail. Audacious people succeed partly because they are aware and able to consider and value relationships. The situation is even worse for an organisation that inhibits the sympathy state in its employees. This is because it is unlikely to be characterised by the rich, supportive relationships that enable people to feel able to take risks, make mistakes and take the personal responsibility needed to react quickly to unfolding events.

Identification: me versus you

The last domain is that of *identification*, or who it is that we are focusing our other motivational states on. The two elements here are *me* and *you*. 'You' is any other person or thing that we identify with in a motivational state as not us. Again, it seems as if we need one to define the other in normal human activity. For a long time, it was argued in psychology that young babies could not differentiate themselves from the rest of the world.

However, the eminent psychologist Margaret Donaldson has argued from evidence of controlling and predicting behaviour in babies that:

> If a baby gets satisfaction from learning to predict events in the world and to control them, then presumably she has some conception of a world 'out there' to be controlled. And by the same token presumably she has some conception of *herself* as a controlling agent.[13]

Part of our growing up is to build upon this distinction to be able increasingly to see the world from two viewpoints. This can be represented as shown in Figure 3.7.

The self-oriented state (G) is the motivational state being experienced when you are focused on 'me'. Clearly, in this state we view our actions in terms of how they relate to ourselves, whether this is in terms of being in control or being liked. What we value is individuation: the sense of personal responsibility, self-worth.

The contrast to this state is, unsurprisingly, the other-oriented state (H), where motivational needs are met by the success and well-being of others. There is a transcendent quality value to this state, whereby the feeling of self is sublimated into the service of another, whether that is another individual such as a child or partner, an organisation or even a spiritual entity.

These last two domains provide good examples of how the domains work as a whole. For example, when we are in the self-oriented and sympathy states it is ourselves that we want to feel cared for and loved. In the other-oriented (you) and mastery states we want someone else to be in control, whether that is a child learning to ride a bike or someone at work developing a new skill. The point is that the many combinations of states are experienced in different ways, with significant implications for audacity (Table 3.1).

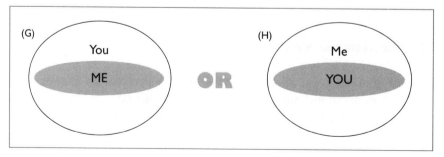

Figure 3.7 'Me' and 'you' in the identification domain

	Table 3.1 Summary of motivational states and their implications for audacity	
Motivational state	**Experienced as**	**Implications for audacity and risk-taking**
Serious	Focus on goals, achievement, direction, planning, risk-conscious.	Can provide the vision of something that must be achieved. If we feel the goals are in doubt can cause anxiety.
Playful	Focus on experimenting, trying things out, creativity, open thinking, and intrinsic pleasure of the activity or job itself.	Enjoyment of the ambiguity of a situation. Threat is experienced as something exciting, can enhance experience of the other states.
Conforming	Focus on implementation, following agreements and processes, a concern for maintenance and routines.	Positively, it can provide efficiency as proven approaches and methods are used. Less positively, it encourages the conventional and a lack of questioning.
Rebellious	Focus on being different, challenging, breaking conventions, critical analysis and conflict.	The well-spring need to break away and do something different. The basis of our curiosity and need to challenge the accepted.
Mastery	Wanting oneself, the team or the organisation to succeed. Focus on building up the power and resources of oneself and others.	The key to confidence in risk-taking: the more you feel control and the greater the uncertainty the better you feel! Encourages a search for capability.
Sympathy	Focus on building harmony and good interpersonal working relations, wanting to co-operate and showing empathy. Wanting to support and be supported.	Risk involving people requires this perspective. Danger of mastery is that we turn people, even ourselves into objects. Also often the real risk in risk-taking is people's reaction.
Self-oriented	Focus on personal success and a willingness to take responsibility, control and master new challenges. Willingness to be in the limelight.	The willingness to accept responsibility is pivotal in risk-taking. Self coupled with mastery, offers pride or humiliation. Self-sympathy is feeling sorry for yourself.
Other-oriented	Focus on guiding and caring for others, willingness to sacrifice own needs for others. Team spirit.	Much audacity requires a team of people; this state means we pay attention to others. At times we may need to cut ourselves off from some.

One of the central arguments of this book is that all eight states are required for audacity. But what is true is that not all eight states are experienced equally. In the examples of audacity that have been highlighted so far you could expect that if the road to audacity requires a love of the journey, a sense of wilfulness and power to face up to the challenge, then consequently the motivational states of playfulness, rebelliousness and mastery associated with self are really going to matter. And we find in all sorts of ways that these are states that are more experienced in general by those exhibiting behaviour that might be called audacious.

As you might have already gathered from the above descriptions of the states, it is precisely these states – particularly the first two – that can be most inhibited in an organisation and attract the most criticism. These issues will be returned to later, but first of all we need to be clear on how the general experience of a state links itself to particular activity in the world because this has important consequences for the way we understand how a particular thing will motivate us to change course or do something new.

Connecting to audacity

How do these states connect to behaviour, and in particular how do these states connect to *audacious* behaviour? What seems to be the case is that we represent success or satisfaction in each of these states with a kind of plan or connection, a way of translating our motivational states into action that will satisfy them.

For example, in the serious state, one person might represent success as achieving the maximum wealth they can, whereas for another it is about having enough to live on to do other things. Success may be to gain a promotion or to discover a drug that will save millions of lives. For a long time, the only success I (Steve Carter) could imagine was to play very loud guitar in a successful rock band – not, as it turned out, a particularly viable strategy!

In a sympathy state, one might see satisfaction in having a very deep and intense relationship with one or two people, expressed through quiet moments together, or one might see it through a much larger group of people and noisier and livelier activity.

For want of a better phrase we can think of these connections as 'private strategies', and they are a bit like the Adlerian idea of a private logic or Kelly's personal construct. Both of these writers see the way we deal with the world as arising from within an individual, and are only indirectly related to external expectations. There can be something wonderfully idio-syncratic about this. An old psychology lecturer of mine expressed his mastery state through learning a new language every year; I believe that he was approaching twenty languages when I last heard about him. He rarely if ever published a psychology paper.

Within a motivational state, private strategies will determine what someone finds as important. Manifestly, being in a serious state does not determine completely what a person will find important, pay attention to, or try to obtain. This is why motivation is such a difficult issue for leaders and why lists of things that motivate people as found in many management articles are so problematical.

For example, 'development' is postulated as a good motivator of people. And it is. However, it would probably be most relevant when someone was in a mastery state (except for those who go on courses to make friends) and would be less so at a particular moment if you were in a rebellious state. However, even in a mastery state it might be less successful if my private mastery strategy saw 'development' opportunities as something that might expose my uncertainty – my mastery strategy might be avoid any activity that might expose me to ridicule.

An important insight that I have gained from profiling the amount of time individuals, particularly managers, spend in each state, is that they can differ hugely. It often seems that if someone spends a little time in a particular state then they lack a strategy that works for them in that state. A poignant example of this is talking to men who find that they don't know how to love their children. By this I don't mean that they do not love their children, but rather that they find it very hard to act in a way that allows them to get satisfaction from their needs in this state. In one case, a man kept trying to play with his kids, and to his horror and guilt found that he got bored or frustrated. The problem here is that he had not found a viable strategy to be able to get the rewards that would sustain him in that particular state.

Viability is an essential qualification. There needs to be a balance between the state, the way it is manifest and the circumstances in which activity takes place. In the example of the father and his children, clearly a lack of an adequate expression of love meant that no connection could be made. Alternatively, we could have a very strong strategy, such as 'I am going to climb Everest'; however, given the circumstances of my fitness levels and complete lack of experience, my strategy can hardly be said to be viable.

It is likely (and a subject for another book) that the viability of strategies is something that forms part of our development, and that as our circumstances and environmental demands change we need to build new strategies to deal with the world. The limited development or lack of viable strategies is what may inhibit the expression of motivational states later in life.

For example, parenting, which is full of 'should' and 'ought' and 'why don't you', may result in an individual finding it difficult to develop viable strategies later in life for the self (me) and mastery states. In turn, this would inhibit personal responsibility and the initiation of change. This would be especially true in organisations that maintain this parenting role through rules, procedures and conformity.

Now, the converse is true of audacity.

Audacious people seem to have developed strategies enabling them to maximise the rewards from highly uncertain situations. As we said earlier, initially this is because they can involve themselves positively with high arousal. Through this, they can achieve heightened rewards in many, if not all the other states. Time and again, in my experience audacious people channel the excitement and exhilaration of risk into all their eight ways of being, revelling in being – as my daughter would say – 'full on'.

Anyone seeking a more audacious life has to begin by asking: 'What strategies do I have that will enable me to connect all eight motivational states that make up who I am to the opportunities of uncertainty?'

Organisations seeking greater audacity first need to ask: 'How do we get our people to motivationally connect with our businesses so that the uncertainty we face is seen as a source of reward?'

In developing this I am arguing that organisations need to place the way they help individuals connect to them motivationally, particularly focusing on those motivational states that are historically inhibited by organisational life but that are essential to audacity.

The organisations that we belong to and work for are, as we have seen, a key determinant of the viability of the strategies that we hold about living a motivationally rich life. They can inhibit or promote the circumstances that surround them. They can also, through leadership and coaching, develop and enhance individual strategies. These will be the subject of further discussion in Chapter 5.

This chapter has dealt with a rich and powerful account of who we are and how audacity plays a role within this. The first two challenges to understanding how to be successfully audacious have thus been addressed. Motivational connection alone, however, does not mean we can deal successfully with uncertainty. One question remains: How do we cope successfully with the threat that lies in wait for us amid uncertainty? If we can answer this, then we are in a position to face our third challenge – to start down the road to audacity.

Notes

1   Hebb, D.O. (1955) Drives and the C.N.S. (Conceptual Nervous System), *Psychological Review*, **36**

2   Walters, J., Apter, M.J. and Svebak, S. (1982) Colour Preference, Arousal and the Theory of Psychological Reversals, *Motivation and Emotion*, **6**

3 Lafreniere, K.D., Cowles, M.P. and Apter, M.J. (1988) The Reversal Phenomenon: Reflections on a Laboratory Study, in Apter, M.J., Kerr, J.H. and Cowles, M.P. (eds), *Progress in Reversal Theory*, Elsevier, Amsterdam

4 In this review of reversal theory I (Steve Carter) am developing the arguments within the structure outlined. This approach is one that I have found powerful particularly when considering the idea of audacity. In doing so, however, the reader should be aware that I am not following the 'orthodox' route into the theory. The language of the theory is precise and technical, and for the general reader the wording and concepts used here may be more helpful. In particular, the language and notions around 'aspects of experience' are my own. A full technical description of the theory can be found in Apter, M.J. (ed.) (2001) *Motivational Styles in Everyday Life*. American Psychological Association, Washington DC

5 Ibid.

6 Stark, F. (2001) *The Valley of the Assassins*, Modern Library Paperbacks, New York (first pub. 1934)

7 Phillips, A. (1999) *Saying No*, Faber and Faber, London

8 Durkheim, E. (1951) *Suicide*, Free Press, New York (first pub. 1897)

9 Mitchell, Jr. R.G. (1988) The Sociological Implications of the Flow Experience, in Csikszentmilhalyi, M. and Csikszentmilhalyi, I.S. (eds) *Optimal Experience*, Cambridge University Press, Cambridge

10 De Botton, A. (2000) *The Consolations of Philosophy*, Penguin Books, London

11 Kerr, J. and Apter, M.J. (1991) *Adult Play – A Reversal Theory Approach*, Swets and Zeitlinger, Amsterdam

12 O'Connell, K. and Brooks, E. (1997) In Svebak, S. and Apter, M.J. (eds), *Stress and Health – A Reversal Theory Perspective,* Taylor and Francis, Bristol

13 Donaldson, M. (1992) *Human Minds – An Exploration*, Penguin, London

CHAPTER FOUR

The Meaning of Mountains

Steve Venables has been described as one of the most talented climbers of his generation – and one of the most articulate. He was one of the first Britons to climb Everest without oxygen, reaching the summit on his own in May 1988. In doing so, he pioneered with a small team a remarkable new route up the Kanshung face, the biggest wall on Everest. It has been a privilege to have met and worked with Steve many times over the last ten years and our conversations were one of the inspirations behind this book.

The 'real' dangerous edge

Climbing, on the face of it, is wilfully perverse. The deliberate seeking of that balancing point where a split second of inattention, the collapse of a piece of faulty equipment made late on a Friday afternoon or a capricious change in the weather can lead to a spectacular death, challenges us to wonder just what we are playing at. Attributing this wilfulness merely to the existence of these grand landscapes – or 'because they are there' – is a sop to the ground-locked. It is as if the complexity of the 'whyness' of it makes us inarticulate. There is a special motivational richness and complexity to the ascent of the world's great peaks, accessible to those who have the 'protective frame' (a concept explored more fully in the next chapter) to experience the challenge as exciting rather than terrifying. This makes them wonderful examples of the 'motivational connectedness' we have just discussed.

Listening to Steve Venables talk about his challenges to groups of managers over the years and seeing their reaction, I was always struck by how powerfully his stories hit home. At one level listeners were just in awe of the skill and courage of climbers and explorers who are prepared to go to the extreme limits of human endurance and return again for more. People were quite happy to acknowledge that this is something they could admire and applaud, be thrilled by – from a distance. At another level people would connect in a powerful, inarticulate way that moved some of them to tears and others into a deep and thoughtful reflection about themselves. After a while I came to realise that people were seeing something about their own condition. Not in a pretentious, self-deluding way, but through recognising in a distilled and extremely focused form some of the choices, paradoxes and opportunities of their own lives. Reversal theory gave structure and insight to these issues.

Mountains and reversal theory

The first insight was into our relationship with what we are doing, the distinction between *serious* or *playful*. Are we going to do things for some future reward or benefit, or should we do them purely for their own, immediate, intrinsic reward? Do we fall into the trap of treating the world too seriously, always chasing some future goal and never enjoying the journey or the present? Do we spend too much time seeking excitement and interest, so at times we feel aimless and our lives lacking purpose?

Often, listening to Steve left people considering how they would face up to threat. How would you face up to the 'dangerous edge'? Hanging by your fingertips as you struggle round an overhang is thrilling and exciting if you are in a confident, *playful* state and totally absorbed in the here and now. Whereas in a *serious* state, being over-anxious about the consequences of a fall can reduce you to gibbering terror. We can only be in the *playful* state in these circumstances when we have a protective frame of reference, based upon a sense of confidence in our own competence, colleagues and equipment.

It is this protective frame or lack of it that distinguishes the mountaineer from the view-seeker. This is not to suggest that a climber is never *serious*, nor that he or she never loses the protective frame: they can degenerate into pure funk like everyone else. Moreover, *seriousness* is vital sometimes to plan ahead and anticipate problems. Reaching the summit is a serious, intensely rewarding, goal. The point is that they have the ability to feel *playful* with 5,000 feet of space beneath their feet! *Serious* or *playful* – good climbers have two ways to win on a mountain.

But that was not the end of it. The questions raised by any consideration of the why of climbing also involve the impact of the other three pairs of states. For instance, what is to be the balance in our lives between *fitting in* and *breaking free*? Humans orient themselves instinctively towards the assumptions and expectations of the group of people they associate with. Most of us value the security of belonging, fitting in, conforming; but we can also relish the passion of being the rebel, the radical, the mould-breaker. This polarity applies particularly to climbers. Most climbers enjoy being a member of that idiosyncratic club of committed mountaineers and, for example, the historical resonance of repeating a great, classic, well-known climb. But also in Steve's memorable phrase, which was nearly the sub-title of this book, many also find great reward from the chance to 'draw a new line up the side of a mountain'. For the audacious, the curious and the questioning, not many things are more rewarding than literally or metaphorically going where no one has been before. Of course, this is always risky, and many artists, scientists, explorers and even business people have paid a heavy price for doing so. Not to break new ground, however, is to deny an important part of who we are.

Learning from the journey

The greatest misconception about climbing is that it is solely about achieving the summit. Many climbers will tell you that some of their most rewarding climbs were the ones where they did not meet the summit but instead gained some learning, some new conundrum understood and some profound insight into their craft mastered. This relates to the third pair of states proposed by Michael Apter in reversal theory. The immense sense of reward that *mastery* offers with its associated feelings of dominance, getting in control of a situation is central to encouraging us to push ourselves forward. One of the greatest gifts a parent or teacher can give a child is to give them confidence: confidence in things in general, confidence in things specifically, confidence in themselves and confidence in others. Sometimes the confidence and competence of others can cause jealousy. It may be the basis of rivalry but at other times it can be a basis for real pleasure.

Venables climbed Everest with only three others and a small support team. Both teams were too small, in the opinion of many experts. This close-knit, wilful group allowed a real pride in others to develop; mastery experienced alongside the 'other' rather than the 'self' state.

He [Ed Webster] had never climbed overhanging ice before, but at 6,600 metres on Everest was as good a place as any to learn. It was a masterly performance. First he took off his rucksack and left it on a ledge. Now without the weight of the sack, he could at least stay in balance for the first moves up a little ramp which leaned rightwards into the cliff. He moved confidently up this, placed an ice screw, climbed higher, then placed another ice screw, clipped in a footloop and used this to surmount an overhanging bulge. Then he moved back left, like some spidery crab spread-eagled on four clawed legs. The most impressive part was the speed and skill in which he placed ice-screws, whilst hanging so precariously from one ice hammer.[1]

As we have already outlined, sharing in an adventure with a team we can be proud of can be immensely important. Often within this team a close bond with others will also grow, and support and friendship are given and received within the sympathy state.

Successful climbers tend to be very self-contained. They are often not obvious team players and yet in the right circumstances they relish the affection, openness and trust that can exist between people. Holed up with one or two others in a tent through a four-day blizzard requires the participation of people who genuinely enjoy company and friendship for its own sake.

So climbing can be about learning and a sense of *power*, or it can be about *strong relationships*. Implicit in the way we experience this is Apter's fourth pair of ways of experiencing the world. Are we seeing a particular situation in terms of ourselves or others? Is it *our* feelings and success that matter, or is it the success of *someone else* (or the team as a whole)? It would be a dishonest climber who would claim never to have been switching back and forward from one's own needs to those of others.

This complexity and paradox is at the heart of the most important aspect of climbing and a further clue to its motivational richness – the relationships within a team. The tension between these two tendencies is a common experience for individuals in extreme circumstances. Do I stay and help the weaker struggling team member, or should I provide impetus by forging ahead? If it came to it, would I leave a dying climber behind to save my own skin? Most climbers are mercifully spared that terrible choice, but there is a constant crossing of the self–other divide. A ruthless ability to concentrate solely upon oneself and one's needs and success can be a huge asset, provided it is tempered with the ability, at times, to value and nurture your companions.

On Everest, after months of working together, the last assault on the summit was made by the team with each member tackling the challenge on their own. Only Venables made it to the top. On the morning of the last day they had set off roped together, although previously this had not been the plan. Venables was sceptical about how useful the rope would be, but said nothing.

The companionship in our tent had been so good that day that I did not want to shatter it by refusing this symbolic link.

Later, however, he became frustrated, as the rope was causing him to lose momentum.

Soon after midnight, I shouted down, 'It's no good. We need to go faster and the rope's just a nuisance – just another thing to trip up on and no-one's going to fall off here.' There was some muttering below and I think that Robert said, 'Yes, I agree – we should unrope.' I said that I would trail the rope ready to be used higher up if necessary.

Perhaps it was selfish of me to push on alone, as if rejecting the friendship and teamwork which had sustained this expedition for nearly three months. However, we had always known that on this final stretch we would be unlikely to move at the same speed or to use a rope effectively... on this occasion I was determined to give myself every possible chance of success.

I have heard Steve Venables talk about this dilemma many times and watched as people rehearsed in their own minds the 'solution'. It seems to crystallise perfectly the paradox of who we are. It is essentially a *motivational* dilemma, and your 'solution' will be almost completely determined by your own motivational state when you consider it.

A motivationally rich promise

So this is the rich promise of mountains – the chance to work seriously towards some intensely stimulating vision of goals, to enjoy highs of intense exhilaration, to become a member of a special and closely knit club bound by mutual understanding. But it is also the promise to strike out on one's own and defy expectations, to learn and go on learning, to understand oneself more intensely and at the same time to feel part of something bigger. Not all climbers experience all of these states equally, although the theory would suggest that they do experience all of them to some extent. Few care to verbalise their experiences too precisely, and most are tempted to follow the example of George Mallory, fobbing off the inquisitors with a cavalier 'because it's there'.

Note

1   Venables, S. (1999) *Everest, Alone at the Summit*, Odyssey Books, London (first pub. 1989)

CHAPTER FIVE

Walking the Dangerous Edge

How can we be audacious?

We have seen that the reward for audacity at an individual level is heightened reward in all of the eight states of our being. Whether focused on mastery or sympathy, being serious or playful, rebelling or conforming, concerned with oneself or others, audacity has a role to play. Organisationally, audacity allows us to enter those areas where value can be created through innovation, differentiation and decisive action.

That is why audacity matters. But *how* can we achieve this? How do we capture the benefits from those eight states when faced with the threats of the unknown, unavoidable or sometimes deliberately sought? How do we avoid anxiety and experience excitement?

This chapter explains how we can successfully deal with uncertainty, how to walk the dangerous edge between security and disaster. In doing so, it deals with two fundamental aspects of performance: confidence and awareness. A good starting point in exploring how to be audacious is the notion of the *dangerous edge* – an important concept within reversal theory.

Stepping up to the dangerous edge

By now, we hope you accept the idea that people are not eternally and entirely risk-avoiding. In taking risks, however, it is not that we are unaware of the dangers in principle, it is just that we don't really believe that we will come to harm. We focus instead on a whole variety of pleasures arising from mastery, playfulness, sympathy and rebelliousness in a heightened state. This situation of increasing arousal is represented in Figure 5.1.

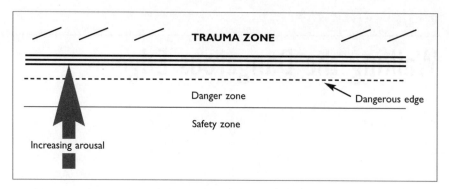

Figure 5.1 The dangerous edge

This is another example of the figure and ground phenomenon. We need to feel the presence of danger but not to focus on it. The trauma zone is where harm is done, and the harm may be physical, financial, reputational or in some other form. Or it may be psychological, resulting in feelings such as humiliation or embarrassment. It is represented in almost any human activity, for example the ruinous critical review of a new play, the marketing campaign that leaves everyone cold, the major project that goes way over time and budget. It is the potential for disaster on a mountain climb or on the high seas; it is the product launch that fails or the presentation that goes humiliatingly wrong. Trauma doesn't have to be as large as this, the consequence being that not every activity has the same potential for excitement.

Trauma is perceived as threatening, and at a basic physiological level it is arousing. How we respond to this will depend upon whether we are in a serious, arousal-avoiding state, or in a playful, arousal-seeking state.

In a serious state we have a choice: either we retreat from the 'edge' to the safety zone, or we try and cope with our fears and hang on in the danger zone, all the time feeling anxious and stressed about anything that moves us towards the edge. It is as if we were tied to a piece of elastic, all the time trying to pull us back to safety. This is the reason why when the going gets tough, the tough sometimes give up.

The problem, organisationally, is that it is often at the edge that value is created. Individually too, it often represents the point of highest performance. A good friend of mine and a great tennis coach put it this way: 'When serving at 40-all what is going through your mind? For some it is "I mustn't serve a double-fault" and for others "Can I hit an ace?" It is the latter that go on to be winners.'

Organisationally, I have come across one or two organisations that I have come to see as 'arousal flirts'. They launch new initiatives, bold moves focused on new markets or new positioning, and then when things don't go according to plan retreat back to the safety zone to think of new plans and initiatives. Of course, it could be that the new idea was wrong and it makes complete sense to give up in the face of better market knowledge – but when it becomes a pattern of behaviour are we seeing a reality or a pathology?

In the arousal-seeking playful state, the pull is in a different direction. It is towards the edge. How is that we can deal with threat and the potential for a trauma in this way? According to reversal theory, it is because at times we see the world from within a psychological 'protective frame'. This is an essential landmark on the road to audacity. It is a way of being within a highly aroused state, but in such a way that the consequences of falling over the edge are removed or downplayed to a point of little consequence.

In the safety zone it is easy. The protective frame we experience is a safety frame, a sense that we can observe danger but not get caught up in it. We position ourselves far enough from the edge to feel no real threat. It is like standing behind the safety rail on a high cliff by the sea listening to the roar of enormous waves. The excitement is there but from a distance. The buzz is real and the experience stimulating. Protective frames, however, are psychological phenomena – ways of seeing the world – which may or may not match objective reality.

I remember gathering with some friends at Robin Hood's Bay, a village on the east coast of England. It was early January and a fierce storm had been raging in the North Sea for several days. The tiny harbour lay at the bottom of two steeply inclined narrow streets, and although the rain had stopped and the wind had lessened slightly, huge waves were crashing into the buildings standing close to the harbour's edge, with icy spray flying up into the air over them. The harbour has a slipway at its right hand side and to the left is a level area a few metres above the water line at low tide. A white wooden fence had been constructed, presumably to stop summer holidaymakers falling in the sea. We gathered some way back from the fence and cheered each crashing wave, relishing the spray on our faces and the roaring explosive thunder of breaking seawater. Behind the fence and some way back from the edge we all felt safe.

The fence marked a margin of our safety frame.

Suddenly, a maverick wave hit the harbour and the wooden fence was splintered into pieces of matchwood. Instinctively, we all turned and fled back up the road, for an instant completely panic-stricken before reaching safety and dissolving into hysterical laughter. From a reversal theory viewpoint the illusion of safety was enough for us to be exhilarated by the power of nature. The abrupt removal of the physical representation of safety, the fence, caused an instant reversal from exhilaration to high anxiety and a flight to safety. Whereupon we could resume being in the playful state as our protective frame was now restored because of our distance from the sea. The important and rueful thing to note was not whether or not we were in any real danger – it was our perception that counted. The fence represented a dangerous edge that was suddenly rushing towards us!

The safety frame is something that we can build into our situation. To build a safety frame requires only that you can cut off the onlooker from the serious consequences of stepping over the dangerous edge. By focusing on the immediate situation and cutting ourselves off from the world with all its uncertainties, we are able to enjoy being close to threat and uncertainty. Sporting stadia are built to enclose us in this protected space, and that is why the best ones create such an exciting atmosphere. Casinos are rarely designed with windows providing a view on to an outside world, disconnecting us psychologically from malevolent reality. Food and drink are often brought in to casino players to maintain distancing from reality. Mary Gerkovitch[1] has highlighted the way that the lights, music and costuming of casino staff all contribute to the feeling of disconnection from consequence. She points out that using chips instead of real money makes it feel more like a game for fun without any real impact, obscuring the real losses being experienced.

In this safety frame we can live life to the motivational full, subtly and falsely removed from the consequences.

And, of course, the same is true of a financial trading floor.

The first time I went on a trading floor, where hundreds of analysts and traders worked every day, I was struck by the serried rows of computer screens resembling one-armed bandits, the shaded windows, the food at the desk, the 'dressing up' – how much it reminded me of less salubrious places one might visit. The trading floor is a place that has been designed to play in. More than one of the people I have got to know in this industry has talked about working there as 'playing a game', having a good 'innings', 'scoring a good goal'.

This is not necessarily a bad thing. As we have seen, being in the playful state can often be associated with superior problem-solving and productivity. For reasons that we will discuss later in this chapter, high-pressure challenges may be best faced when mastery is a strongly experienced state. The mastery state makes winning important for its own sake, not for any more important reason. It is about demonstrating capability. Its rewards are feelings of power and control; for example, it encourages traders to develop the individual resources they need to succeed. It may well be impossible in the pace and high drama of a dealing room to cope if you were largely and dominantly in a serious state. The likelihood is that you would burn out with high-anxiety stress.

Of course, for traders this all works very well in the good times (such as the late 1980s and late 1990s), but sometimes unwelcome reality comes bursting through the shaded windows and monitors, excitement turns to panic, individuals and groups no longer operate within a protective frame. Traders unfamiliar with these conditions can over-react, taking things too seriously and filling the financial papers with gloomy articles about the mood and mindset of the 'market'. In fact, financial trading provides a perfect example of the subjective nature of risk – an example that is quickly forgotten in the good times, when risk once again becomes something that can be managed and controlled by clever insight and analysis.

The confidence frame and the England middle order batting collapse

The 'safety' frame is of course most obviously the one associated with the perception of being at a distance from perceived trauma. However, another protective frame that allows us to approach much closer to the dangerous edge yet still find arousal exciting is the confidence frame (Figure 5.2). This is a psychological frame of reference in which we feel in control of what is going on, even while acknowledging the presence of danger. This confidence can come from within ourselves, from our team mates or the equipment we are using.

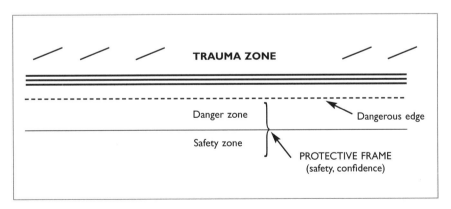

Figure 5.2 Protective frames

Experiencing life within a confidence frame is one of its most rewarding benefits. One of my earliest memories is of my father helping me to learn to ride a bicycle on a cinder track at a local park. The bicycle seemed big and awkward, and previous outings on the cinder had taught me its stinging potential to graze knees, elbows and palms. I was seriously aware of the consequences of falling off.

But this was to be the day. Stabilisers were taken off. We had some trial runs, with my father gamely running to hold the seat and keep me upright. This, backbreaking for him, activity made me feel secure. So much so that instead of focusing on avoiding disaster, I relaxed a bit, sped up, started to enjoy the rhythm of the wheels and the sensation of speed. All of a sudden, I realised that my father, either deliberately or because his back was aching, had let go. For a perilous moment I panicked, anticipated disaster and wobbled dangerously. Somehow the momentum of the bicycle kept me going and I started pedalling again. I was cycling! I felt in control, and, freed from the fear of imminent disaster, I was playfully and completely immersed in the moment, enjoying the experience of what I was doing. So much so that even now, years later, I can remember the sound of the wheels crunching over the cinders, the sun making patterns on the whirring spokes, the feel of the wind rushing over my face. I recall dangerously watching the chain of the cycle engaging and disengaging with the cogs of the pedal.

Confidence here is largely but not exclusively about self-mastery. Success in these two states enables a confidence frame that allows us to contribute fully to any organisation, to live a full life. It is the basis upon which organisations can take full advantage of an uncertain world. The 'other' ('you') state can also be involved, in that we can work to make others competent and thus confident – important, of course, when we are working in a team or relying on others. The knock-on effect is that working with others who are confident often gives us personally a sense of control.[2]

The confidence frame is a fundamental part of audacity. Diagnosing where individuals or organisations lack confidence is an essential part of better risk-taking.

But confidence in what?

The above examples are about confidence born of capability. Confidence can also come from information we have received or calculated about the level of threat. It is the statistical likelihood that something may or may not happen, or that a specific need in a particular state may be met. This suggests that there are two basic types: confidence in something happening or not, and confidence in ourselves being able to deal with it. You could call this risk awareness versus risk management. We have already seen that there is something intrinsically flawed about calculating risk when human agency is involved. Yet confidence frames are often predicated upon quantitative analysis of risk; from governments to individuals, we turn to numbers as a way of building confidence. For example, we are encouraged to inoculate ourselves and our family because the chances of an adverse reaction to the drug are only 'one in a million'.

This is self-evidently the psychological role of risk analysis and our wish to make risk objective and quantifiable. Of course, it is reasonable and rational to want to try and understand the nature of risk. However, as writers about risk such as Adams and Taleb have proposed, we have an almost unquenchable need to believe that risk is something definable and controllable, despite evidence that this may often be a futile hope.

Why is this? Because we take risk seriously.

In a serious state of mind any ambiguity is a threat and, of course, unpleasant. Psychologically reducing the threat by rationalising and defining it as 'less-threat' is an understandable strategy. However, this doesn't make for successful audacity. Later on, we will discuss the role of awareness within audacity; for the time being we would argue that denying the threat is an ineffective response to uncertainty. Instead, we should concentrate on how we enable ourselves to deal with it audaciously. To do this, we need to develop perspectives much more based upon the mastery and playful states, and indeed the rebellious and other states as well. The confidence frame needs to be built on firmer foundations than knowing the odds.

Trying to deal with risk in a serious mindset only, is in itself a risky and health-harming strategy. It often builds in its own seeds of failure. We have termed this phenomena the *English Middle Order Batting Collapse*. For those of you unfamiliar with the arcane and perplexing English game of cricket (including, it would seem, some of the team), all you need to know is that 11 players from one team attempt to score as many runs (points) as possible, while the other side try and get them out by various obvious and less obvious means. The English side – particularly when playing the Australians – usually follows a depressingly familiar pattern when attempting to build a big score. The first one, two or three players do only moderately well; players four through eight do desperately badly, and the last three players put up a heroic but ultimately futile fight, scoring more runs than the supposedly better-quality batsmen in the middle of the team. It's enough to make you want to take up baseball.

Why does this happen? Could it be that the middle order are taking the game too seriously? Coming in to bat with a history of failure behind them, these batsmen have a very clear goal: to score enough to make sure they build a winning position. Their heads are full of the *consequences* of what they are doing, rather than what they are doing itself. Indeed, they may be thinking specifically of the consequences of failure (future orientation is a symptom of the serious state). Sven Svebak, the Norwegian physiologist, has shown that in a serious state not only do we feel anxiety but also our muscles tense up and quickly get tired. It is extremely likely, in the very uncertain position of having an Aussie bowler trying to remove your head with a hard cricket ball travelling at 100 miles per hour, that your physical performance will be impaired.

Now, the last batsmen in have no such problems. Being specialists in bowling not batting, there are no expectations that they should make a contribution of any size to the score. The consequences of failure at a personal level are small and, relieved of these serious demands, they often seem to enjoy the freedom, succeeding where their more competent teammates have failed.

But why doesn't this happen to the Australians?

Our hypothesis would be that the Australians bat from a completely different motivational standpoint. What is most dominant for them is the mastery state. They bat from a mindset of power, control and wanting to dominate the bowling. Often this is 'playfully' for its own sake. Their focus is not on the consequence of what they are doing, but on the thrill of hitting the ball and scoring runs. In a sense, their focus stays within the pitch and on the here and now. They could be playing the game simply and, literally, more playfully. To be able to do this, your protective frame – the confidence frame – has to be on your own strengths and those of your team members. This is why it is so important that in team situations there are high levels of trust among team members.

We are not arguing here, of course, that the English cricket team play all the time in a state of serious anxiety, or that the Australians play in a state of red-blooded mastery. It just seems that way most of the time. Both sides are quite capable of moving between pairs of states that are more salient, as well as reversing between states. Nor are we arguing that being motivated in the serious state does not make an enormous contribution to success. Yet without the confidence frame that arises from having mastery present for much of the time, access to the playful state is denied and the energy implicit in risk and uncertainty is switched off. We can be confident in the serious state, although its rewards are different from those in the playful state and are based upon a relaxed view that the future is about to unfold as it should.

Switching between states: fracturing the protective frame

Reversal theory does not claim that the protective frame is in place for the whole of a particular experience. We usually reverse between the serious and playful states, experiencing arousal as anxiety-inducing or excitement-provoking as we do so. In a study of gambling, Andersen and Brown[3] showed how in casinos gamblers switched between the serious and playful states quite regularly. Often experiencing an emotional roller coaster, although the dominant state is playful, they often end up in a serious state:

> This state was sometimes induced by losing and sometimes by some reminder of the significance of the sums of money involved in relation to larger (serious) concerns outside of the casino, such as paying the rent or debts.

The example of the adventure park ride at the start of the previous chapter also provides an instance of reversal. However, if no protective frame exists, it is doubtful unless coerced that anyone would feel able to approach the dangerous edge. We should remember that both the confidence and the safety cases of the protective frame are psychological. Their removal and the rise in anxiety can occur at any time, despite years of experience at the dangerous edge.

Joe Simpson is a climber and writer who has experienced the high and lows of his sport. He has nearly been killed and survived extraordinary hardships, powerfully described in his book *Touching the Void*. Yet, still he returns to climbing. In his recent book, however, perhaps the 'protective frame ' is beginning to fracture.

> I felt I was more powerful and probably fitter than Tat [his climbing partner] but he had the cunning of vast experience and that was worth a great deal. We were climbing at the same standard and I was confident that I could accurately assess what we could and could not do. This now put me in an awkward position. I urgently wanted to tell him that we should back off, that the climb was in a very dangerous state, that it was too hard for him. But he was the leader. This was his pitch. His choice and I would have to hope that he would come to the same conclusion. I didn't want to force the issue.[4]

At this stage, the dominant state is undoubtedly of mastery – his and Tat's. However, Simpson is clearly in a serious state: note the focus on consequences. Serious anxiety starts to creep in as he loses confidence in Tat and the overall situation.

'The ice is terrible Tat. It's pouring with water, for God's sake!' He glanced over his shoulder at me. 'Fuck it,' I snapped. 'If you fall we're dead. Simple as that.'
'I won't fall, kid.'
'I don't want to die.'
'I won't fall.'
'Maybe, maybe not,' I shrugged. 'I'm sorry. I'm not taking that risk. OK? I don't want to do this. I don't need this.'

Simpson's next chapter is entitled 'Intimations of Mortality', and the rest of the book has an ongoing questioning of the point of climbing and whether Simpson should continue.

But where does this leave organisations? This is the central question of the next chapter. But for the moment consider this. When faced with uncertainty, either opportunistically or reactively, what does an organisation do? Does it support people and focus them on the playful and mastery states? Does it encourage only seriousness by ladling out goals and plans? Or does it mark out safety zones and build capability?

Establishing protective frames

Audacious individuals no doubt build their own protective frames, although as Phillip Whitehead highlighted in the first chapter, they often have to confront the real possibility of trauma, as with his example of Martin Luther King. Organisations through their culture, climate and leadership style do much to encourage or inhibit the protective frames that enable us lesser mortals to be audacious.

As we have said, audacious individuals build their confidence frames from a sense of self-mastery. This particularly happens in the rebellious state, wilfully defying convention and standing out from the crowd. Audacious people often develop extremely effective strategies in these states. When interviewing audacious people, we have been impressed by the way they seem to exercise control. Most people seem to distinguish between two sorts of control: controlling the situation and controlling one's reaction. Audacious people seem to be able to add a third element to their control strategy: they have really learned how to control the way they contribute to a situation.

Controlling the situation

Control is usually seen as control of a situation and being able to shape how events unfold. The viability of this as a strategy is hugely contingent on the situation itself, as well as the power and authority of the individual or organisation. If we take an industry, it is not inconceivable that one could change the market as a whole. Michael Dell did it when he redefined how PCs were sold and distributed. The example of Dell is an interesting one, highlighting control of an emerging situation.

In 1988, Dell Computer started competing aggressively with the leaders in the personal computing market: IBM and Compaq. Dell's strategy was to provide quality personal computers at low (but not the lowest) price, backed up with friendly and reliable after-sales service. But the real key to Dell's success was to target this product offering carefully by getting to know, in detail, his customers. Large amounts of advertising were placed in new and, at the time, unfashionable magazines read by computer experts, raising his business's profile with this significant group. Combined with this was Dell's direct response advertising methods: in order to get the Dell product catalogue, customers either had to complete a detailed response card, or call a toll-free number where they were asked the same, detailed questions. The Dell phone representatives were highly skilled, trained to ask questions but also to listen to customers, recording their preferences and requirements in detail and then acting on them. Potential customers were flattered at the level of attention they were receiving and responded in droves, enabling Dell to build an enormous database of vital information about each individual prospect and customer. This information was then used to help customers, by tailoring computers and services to each individual need in a way that customers understood and appreciated.

Most often, however, this may well be beyond us. The huge competitive and social changes that sweep across the world are very difficult to shape. So how do we respond? Some companies of course deny anything is happening at all, believing the world to be the same as it ever was as they sail into oblivion. In this sense, they are controlling their reaction.

Controlling reaction

The last point is a commercial version of stoicism or 'what will be will be'. Controlling our reactions is an important decision in establishing a confidence frame. What we are saying is that whatever happens to me, I am confident that it won't harm who I am. At one level this may be simple denial, at another the basis of stress management, at another it can be something much more profound.

We see we have choices on how we perceive a situation. In one way this can be a simple reframing, for example, 'I realise I can't win here', becoming 'but I can build new relationships'.

In another way we can tap into the ultimate freedom to be who we are, movingly identified by Viktor Frankl, through his experiences as a prisoner in concentration camps during World War II.

> Then I spoke of giving life a meaning. They must not lose hope but should keep their courage in the certainty that the hopelessness of our struggle did not detract from its dignity and meaning… Everyone has his own specific vocation or mission in life. Therein he cannot be replaced, nor his life repeated. Thus everyone's task is as unique as is his specific opportunity to implement it.[5]

For many people, realising the element of choice in their reactions is confidence-building liberation. In terms of helping people manage their reactions to uncertainty, it is useful to remember that it is often not the ogres of the present but the ghosts of the past that make someone hesitate. Organisationally, it is the myths and distorted memories that start with the line 'the last time we did this'. Building confidence frames needs also to be about exposing these flawed judgements and letting go of limiting beliefs about the organisation and its people. It is the wilful nature of audacious people to look coolly at these histories and then challenge their relevance.

Controlling contribution

Most organisations don't bury their heads in the sand in face of change and uncertainty. They try and fashion some sort of response. Yet, oddly, at an individual level people often miss this opportunity. They seem to have a thought process that considers only two alternatives:

- Can I stop what's happening or causing something to happen?
- If not, I must learn to cope.

Individually and organisationally we may, first of all, have the opportunity to choose whether to be *involved* or not. Alternatively, if making a contribution is essential, we may have choices about how much control can be exerted over the nature of that contribution – what could be termed the psychological contract – a particular way in which one has to deal with the situation.

Lastly, can someone be more confident in their contribution to the change by developing or improving their competence?

To give an example, I want to sail from England to France. The weather is very unpredictable. I can't control the weather (situation). I have a decision to make (involvement). Taking a chance to go, I can decide the route, either the quickest one, which involves some rather tricky tidal races, or a longer, more straightforward route (contract). Having made my decision, I seek advice from some local sailors on the best way to tackle the conditions in front of me (competence). Much later, unmasted and drifting dangerously, I might consider that to be lost at sea is rather a romantic way to go (reaction)!

At any point, each of these may be more or less viable as a strategy for maintaining confidence. The formula is quite simple – the more a person is in control, the more confident they will feel and the more they will be able to deal positively and proactively with the unknown.

In the previous chapter we highlighted the success of Steve Venables, the prominent and successful Everest mountaineer, who was once asked how he coped with fear. His reply was illuminating:

> I focus on my technique, where my left hand is, where my weight is pulling me [*away from serious consequences to masterful control in the here and now*], what the sequences of moves might be, I think about the times I have succeeded at this sort of challenge before [*mastery through competence*], I immerse myself in the problem.[6] [*mastery through reaction*]

Research by psychologists such as Mihalyi Csikszentmihalyi[7] has suggested that focusing on the immediate situation is essential to performance in situations that paradoxically have high consequences for failure – such as surgery or climbing. Immersing yourself in the moment is a way of establishing a confidence frame in which you can focus upon technique and action in dealing with the situation.

There is probably a useful difference to be drawn here between self-consciousness and self-awareness. The former separates what I am doing from the consequence of it, such that I worry about both at the same time, with potential detrimental effects to my concentration and anxiety levels. With self-awareness attention and activity are merged, then a full concentration can be brought to bear upon the challenge. In reversal theory terms this would suggest the dominance of the *playful* state at this moment, with high arousal being positively experienced. Csikszentmihalyi would call this state *flow*:

> In flow, the self is fully functioning but not aware of itself doing it, and it can use all the attention for the task at hand... then there is a sense that the

outcomes of the activity are in principle under the person's own control...
When self is conscious of itself, not only does it become less efficient but the
experience is usually painful.

The ability to playfully focus on the present and keep the consequences of what we do very much in the background is a powerful way
of dealing with the immediate presence of threat. However, playfully
ignoring the consequences of what we do is clearly not going to sustain
us. What we need to do is shift our awareness as required to deal with
reality as it dances forward.

Awareness

So far we have taken a rather naive view of protective frames, assuming
they are always what we perceive them to be. But what about those occasions in which we feel the safety zone isn't safe, when the bridge under
our feet is truly in danger of collapse? The safety frame isn't safe. Or what
about delusions of immortality, common among the young? Like the
teenage hero who thinks he can control the curve at speed, only to find,
tragically, that his confidence was misplaced.

How do we operate audaciously within protective frames that are valid?
The answer lies in awareness.

One of the great insights into sporting performance over the last few
years has been the understanding of the role of awareness in high performance. Elite athletes seem to have a heightened sense of awareness, not
just of what is going on around them but of their own internal world. Moreover, they seem to be able to change this focus to deal with an unfolding
situation. This situation is described in Figure 5.3.

Nideffer's model is one of concentration and has been used to highlight the role of attention in performance. We can take these ideas
further. Successful, audacious performance depends on a high level of
self-knowledge: How am I doing? What assumptions am I making? How
am I emotionally and motivationally responding to the world? It also
depends upon an external focus, sensing what is going on in the environment and what its impact might be. This is highlighted by the successful
audacity of great generals like Napoleon, who had a brilliant understanding of the topography of the battlefield and an eye for the detail
within it. What is crucial is how self-knowledge of our changing and
dynamic internal world leads us to interpret the broad and narrow
features of our external world.

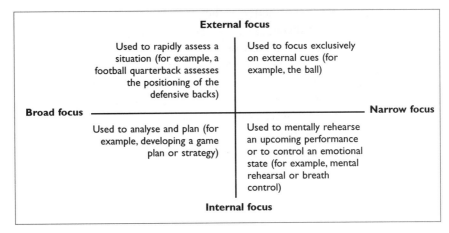

Figure 5.3 Nideffer's model of attentional focus

The Olympic gold medallist and coaching guru David Hemery gives a nice example of how this works in his book *Sporting Excellence*, describing his own event, the 400 metres hurdles.

> For illustration, I will use the 400 metres hurdles to show that performers often use all four types of focus during competition. The hurdler's primary focus of attention is narrow-external, paying attention to the lane and the upcoming hurdle. A broad-internal focus is held to allow the sub-conscious to assess the stride length required to reach the next hurdle in the proper position for a rapid, balanced clearance. In addition to stride length the sub-conscious is taking account of the effects of the wind, track conditions and pace are having on stride pattern for clearing the next hurdle. The performer must also see whether their chosen pace is sufficient to maintain good position against the other competitors. That is using a broad-external focus to consciously assess where one is in relation to all the other competitors in the race. The narrow-internal focus is the personal monitoring of effort and pace judgment.[8]

Almost any sort of audacious activity will require this ability to change attentional focus. A would-be business will need to really understand what its market is doing (broad external), identify specific opportunities to exploit (narrow external), maintain a winning strategy (broad internal) and develop and utilise specific capabilities to achieve it (narrow internal).

What we also need to add to this attentional model is a greater account of the motivational/emotional factors that must be kept in mind: our own and the others around us. Really successful audacity probably requires that we track back and forward between the future-oriented serious state and the here and now playful state, and also that we can harness all eight ways of being and therefore seeing the world to evaluate what is going on. In the pursuit of audacity we need to recognise that what we see from the stand-point of a particular motivational state also inhibits recognising other critical factors. For example, in a mastery state we might not take sufficient account of the emotional impact of what is going on; in the rebellious state we might underestimate the need to be clear on expectations and the need to feel part of something. Powerful awareness will depend upon our motivational versatility – our ability to be in the right state at the right time. And if we are in a team, others will need this ability as well.

Are you with me?

Isabelle Santoire is not tall – yet she is rated by her peers as one of the top climbers in the French Alps. Of the thousand or so guides in the region she is one of only 10 women. Her liberation as a climber came when she realised that her problem was not being shorter than most climbers, but that she was being coached by people who were *taller*. Their awareness of the challenges of rock climbing was informed by conceptions of height and reach. They couldn't see how their way of doing things would work for her. As she acknowledges:

> I saw my problem as not being like them, not being able to provide their solutions to problems. Then I realised what I needed to do was create my own solutions.

This realisation made Isabelle aware that she would have to find her own way of doing things. She now approaches climbing as a series of problems to be solved, rehearsing and re-rehearsing moves and sequences of moves on indoor climbing walls and outside rock faces.

This awareness also works in her favour at an emotional level. When she is on a particularly tricky pitch, one her most frequent questions is 'Are you with me?', directed to the person belaying her and managing the rope that would save her from serious injury if she fell. The question is not just asking 'are you concentrating?' but 'do you see or experience what I am facing?' This level of awareness and rapport is critical in successful climbing, and she seems instinctively to sense when it is not there.

Individual awareness counts for much if we are not to be fooled by false protective frames. It also matters if we are not to miss opportunities by not challenging our assumptions about the true nature of the risk. While some people are more naturally self-aware than others, this is also a skill that can be developed and a discipline to be followed.

How organisations can be aware of an uncertain future

The case of Pierre Wack and Royal Dutch/Shell

In the 1960s, the global energy corporation Royal Dutch/Shell found that its traditional techniques for forecasting cash-flow were inadequate. Hundreds of business units across the world were simultaneously negotiating and servicing contracts and undertaking expensive projects. Although the company had adequate funds and was profitable it was unable to manage its cash effectively, as it did not know – from week to week or even day to day – how much money the company had or how much was needed. Their response was to create a small planning unit to overcome problems of cash-flow management and to forecast future cash requirements. This unit was driven by Pierre Wack, Shell's Head of Group Planning, who soon understood that they were trying to apply statistical techniques to variables that were fundamentally unpredictable.

Wack realised that fundamental uncertainties needed to be distinguished from what could be predicted, and the significance of this extended far beyond cash-flow management (important though this was). So, the group started to discuss the question of what was predictable – in this case, the future of the global oil price and issues of supply and demand. With global demand for oil having grown consistently by 6 per cent to 8 per cent per annum since 1945, demand was initially assumed to be a predetermined factor. This led the team to focus on supply. Given that the engineers assured the group that availability would not be a technical problem, most people in Shell assumed that traditional price trends would continue.

Pierre Wack was not satisfied. He wanted to know if there were other factors in supply, besides technical availability, that might be more uncertain. By listing stakeholders, he quickly arrived at host governments. He posed the questions: Would they be happy to continue to increase production year on year? Would this be in their interest? By playing the role of a major host government, he analysed the policy options available. It soon became apparent that host governments were unlikely to remain amenable to Shell's business activities. Many producing countries did not need an increase in income; they therefore had the upper hand and could exploit the situation to their benefit. In a market of inelastic demand, it would be possible to reduce the volume for supply, knowing that a sharp, accompanying increase in price would more than compensate. The overwhelming logic for the oil-producing countries was to reduce supply, increase prices and conserve their reserves.

When Pierre Wack outlined this to his superiors, he was told that the problem was a lack of unity among oil-producing countries and that, in reality, the oil companies were in control and would do whatever was required to get the volumes needed to satisfy the market. Wack's response was to sharpen the scenario, the conclusions of which were borne out by growth in demand and the increasing realisation by OPEC nations of the strength of their position. As Wack commented:

> Participating in the scenario building process improves a management team's ability to manage uncertainty and risk. Risky decisions become more transparent and key threats and opportunities are identified.[9]

Then, the scenario became reality. The 1973 Israeli-Arab War resulted in a political embargo limiting the supply of oil: prices rose five-fold.

Fortunately for Shell, Pierre Wack's work had encouraged it to prepare and take strategic action well ahead of its competitors. Wack acted audaciously – and persuaded his colleagues to as well – when he realised that change was possible, that his firm had no certain idea of where that change might come from or its possible repercussions, and that this was in itself a colossal risk.

The scenarios that Pierre Wack developed helped Shell's position in the profitability league table of oil companies rise from seventh to second place, and the value for Shell of being ahead of the game was immense. Scenarios remain a vital part of Shell's approach because as current Chairman Philip Watts points out:

> Using scenarios helps us understand the dynamics of the business environment, recognise new opportunities, assess strategic options and take long-term decisions.

Pierre Wack's view was that:

> Scenarios help us to understand today better by imagining tomorrow, increasing the breadth of vision and enabling us to spot change earlier… Effective future thinking brings a reduction in the level of crisis management and improves capability, particularly in change management.

The audacity factor

We have now focused on the three pillars (Figure 5.4) that help someone or some organisation to be audacious. Together they help us specify further the 'audacity factor' that helps businesses and individuals face up to uncertainty.

Motivational connectedness comes through being able to connect the potential of audacity with all eight of the motivational states defined by reversal theory. Through viable private strategies, individuals can connect to the arousing nature and potential of uncertainty. Crucially, to access the states in positive ways in these circumstances requires a protective frame to be in the playful state and to enjoy the arousal. (The serious state, however, provides an important counterbalance in preventing audacity becoming pointless and almost gratuitous.) These protective frames are not made through analysis of the odds but by defining safety zones and building confidence through self-mastery. Finally, the link between our motivation and external circumstances requires the flexibility, attention and focus found in elite athletes.

Organisations that wish to be audacious need to promote all these circumstances. The problem, as we shall see in Chapters 6 and 9, is that many organisations are afraid of their employees and customers, which does make building audacity a challenge.

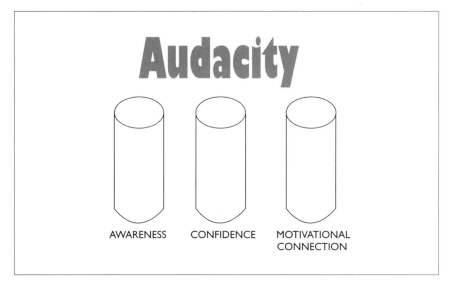

Figure 5.4 The three pillars of audacity

Notes

1 Gerkovitch, M.M. (2001) in Apter, M.J. (ed.), *Risk Taking in Motivational Styles in Everyday Life*, American Psychological Association, Washington DC

2 It should be noted, however, that over-reliance on the mastery of others can induce a kind of learned helplessness, a comfortable place in which we feel relieved of any responsibility to develop confidence in our own individual contributions

3 Andersen, G. and Brown, R.I.F. (1987) Some Applications of Reversal Theory to the Explanation of Gambling and Gambling Addictions, *Journal of Gambling Behaviour*, **3**

4 Simpson, J. (2002) *The Beckoning Silence*, Jonathan Cape, London

5 Frankl, V.E. (1959) *Man's Search For Meaning*, Washington Square Press, New York

6 Venables, S. (1999) *Everest, Alone at the Summit*, Odyssey Books, London

7 Csikszentmihalyi, M. (2002) The Flow Experience and Human Psychology, in *Optimal Experience*, Csikszentmihalyi, M. and Csikszentmihalyi, I.S. (eds), Cambridge University Press, Cambridge

8 Hemery, D. (1991) *Sporting Excellence – What Makes a Champion?*, Collins Willow, London

9 Van der Heijden, K. et al. (2002) *The Sixth Sense*, John Wiley & Sons, Chichester

CHAPTER SIX

Who's Afraid of the Big Bad Employee?

In dealing with volatile, uncertain conditions, how do organisations become audacious? We have argued that audacity requires motivational connectedness – the opportunity to achieve success in a broad range of states; a 'confidence frame' to feel able to access all eight motivational states, and a real awareness of how things are evolving. To talk about 'audacious' organisations, we need to focus on the conditions that foster audacity among their people – after all, organisations are defined, in the end, by the actions of their people.

First, however, it is worth reminding ourselves why the ability to proactively embrace audacity is important: because risk and uncertainty are inevitable. If we accept the axiom that change is the only constant in business, then change leads to uncertainty, uncertainty to risk – and risk requires us to be audacious. In this way, audacity enables us to take control of change.

Organisations need audacity

Organisations need audacity in two ways. First, audacity from their employees means creating new sources of value, meeting the challenges of change and competing. Second, organisations need to be audacious with current and potential customers to generate revenues and profitability, or, in not-for-profit businesses, service. As the volatility curve in Chapter 1 highlights, organisations are not in a position to leave audacity to a few leaders at the top. They need people to take responsibility for unplanned events, unforeseen threats and surprise opportunities.

The problem is that organisations, in the main, are afraid of their people and are afraid of their customers.

This lack of confidence – at times bordering on employee-phobia – results in conditions that inhibit audacity. This inhibition narrows the ways in which employees can feel motivated. Employee-phobic organisations at the worst seem to expect only compliant and dutiful goal-orientation from their employees. This means that they only engage people in two out of the eight motivational states of reversal theory: *serious* and *conforming*. They should not grumble, then, if they only get one quarter of their employees' contribution to productivity and profitability, or if they find contributions like personal responsibility, innovation and renewal hard to obtain. We note with frustration that the UK government's response to the needs for greater levels of productivity, almost inevitably focuses on greater use of targets and new processes (or ways of conforming).

In particular, we would argue that employee-phobic organisations inhibit those areas of motivation that are vital for productivity, innovation, renewal and audacity in particular. The relevant states that are inhibited include playfulness, rebelliousness and the blend of self plus mastery states that focuses an individual on issues of personal control, competence and responsibility.

Research involving nearly 1,600 managers internationally in a variety of industries including the public sector, IT, manufacturing and financial services, found significant differences between the amount of time spent in each of the eight motivational states.[1] These differences are not reflected to nearly the same extent in the general population. Figure 6.1 below clearly shows the difference in serious and playfulness across four sectors; Figure

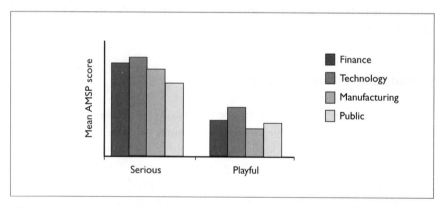

Figure 6.1 Differences in time spent in serious vs. playful motivational states among managers completing the Apter Motivational Style Profile

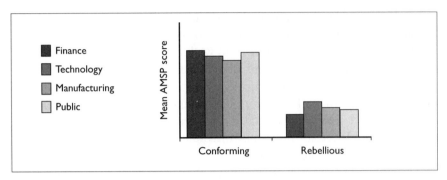

Figure 6.2 Differences in time spent in conforming vs. rebellious
motivational states among managers completing the
Apter Motivational Style Profile

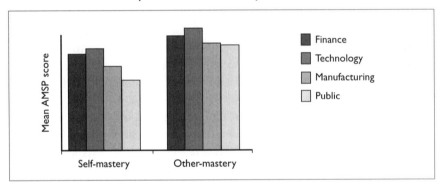

Figure 6.3 Differences in time spent in self-mastery vs. other-mastery
motivational states among managers completing the
Apter Motivational Style Profile

6.2 highlights the difference in the amounts of time spent in the conforming
and rebellious states, and Figure 6.3 shows the less significant but still
important differences in the self-mastery versus other-mastery combinations.

In this chapter, we will explore the basis and solutions of employee-
phobia.

Employee-phobia

Are organisations afraid of their people? The evidence suggests that the
answer is yes, with formal control systems and procedures favoured in
preference to more effective ways of influencing people's behaviours
and actions.

In effect: people are not trusted by organisations.

This matters, because if there is little or no trust then employees' willingness to be bold, take initiatives and walk the dangerous edge leading to genuine value and innovation are all avoided.

The evidence for lack of trust is everywhere. It is in the clauses of employment contracts, for example explaining what gross misconduct is and that it will lead to dismissal, or emphasising the hours of work, or asking the employee to *'undertake any other duties that may be required from time to time'*. To date in my career I have, perhaps foolishly, signed four contracts with employers that have used these words. They could ask me to do anything – and I agreed! The reason I signed them is because I always trusted my new employer to be reasonable; but why did they not understand this and trust me too? Organisations 'agree' targets, budgets, objectives or key performance indicators, with the implication that if these are not achieved then it is the result of poor performance, rather than unexpected change or poor target-setting, and could lead to dismissal. Lack of trust is shown by the process of 'clocking on', with employees required to confirm when they start and when they leave with a time-clock for verification.

As if this lack of trust were not enough, the natural extension of this argument is that because people cannot be trusted – at whatever level they work – they need to be controlled. Hence, the need for budgets, employment contracts, remuneration and audit committees, objectives, appraisals and so forth. People are 'managed', and those doing the managing often have titles of 'directors', executive and non-executive.

In certain call centres (and doubtless other workplaces as well) people are even told how long they can take for a trip to the bathroom, and how many bathroom breaks they can have. Little wonder that managers are then left facing the almost impossible challenge of motivating people and encouraging them to give of their best. If being audacious comes to be seen as taking ten seconds longer to pee, then we are all in trouble.

The effect of all this control tends to inhibit how we gain satisfaction in some states more than others. In particular playfulness is inhibited – people are seen to be mucking about, rebelliousness is inhibited, people are seen to be awkward or even disloyal, and the combinations of states of self and mastery are inhibited; people are seen to be 'out of control', taking decisions without 'authority' and so on. The consequence of this is that the very behaviours a sensible organisation would want people to be motivated to develop are curtailed.

Organisations are in danger of blunting their capacity for audacity, at a time when they need it most.

Malice, laziness and downright corruption

A rather interesting hypothesis you can draw from the implications of changeability highlighted by reversal theory is that the more audacious people are the less they might be trusted. Their wilfulness and clear willingness to do things for their own sake and a confident sense of capability make them more publicly less conforming, perhaps less comfortable to be around. The danger is that the more an organisation seeks audacity the greater will be its fear of its consequences: people taking risks, not following instructions, taking decisions, breaking rules, ignoring hierarchies.

A genie has been let out the bottle.

Why are organisations so nervous about this? We believe that at its heart is a rather myopic confusion of 'inconsistent' behaviour with malice. It reveals an old assumption that people are consistently lazy, shiftless and on the make.

One of the first management gurus, Frederick Taylor, clearly not a believer in the innate value of people, asserted:

> Nineteen out of twenty workmen throughout the civilized world firmly believe it is for their best interests to go slow instead of fast. They firmly believe that it is for their interest to give as little work in return for the money that they get as is practical.[2]

If an organisation takes this view of people then of course what it will do is to make sure it makes every effort to see that everyone does what is expected of them. Henri Fayol is recognised as a founding father of this traditional model, which came into its own around 1910. Fayol developed a set of common activities and principles of management, dividing general management activities into five aspects: planning, organising, commanding, co-ordinating and controlling.

- Planning involves considering the future, deciding the aims of the organisation and developing a plan.
- Organising is the task of marshalling the resources necessary to achieve these aims, as well as structuring the organisation to complete its activities.
- Commanding means achieving the optimum return from people – frequently the most expensive component of a business.
- Co-ordinating is aimed at focusing and particularly unifying people's efforts.

- Control is about monitoring that everything works as planned, adjusting where necessary and feeding this information back so that it can be of value in future planning exercises.

This 'classical' approach is largely concerned with senior managers marshalling and directing resources within organisations. It is characterised by hierarchy, usually in the form of 'top-down' planning and control, formal target-setting and performance measurement, structured programmes for functional improvements through 'scientific' engineering and a formal organisation structure. Fayol can be seen as a fore-runner of modern theorists who take a prescriptive view of management – which seeks the precision of a planned military campaign and ignores the desperately confused execution of that campaign.

An insidious extension to this thinking is that some people need to be controlled (not trusted) and others can be free to be audacious. This is a view that audacity may be fine in theory, but in practice it only works at certain levels. The feeling tends to be that if people are not sufficiently educated or if they are paid modestly, then they are unlikely to respond to an approach intended to develop their individual talents and desire to be audacious. This view promotes workplace discrimination, for example, between more expensive 'white collar' executives, and less expensive, so-called 'blue collar' workers. The problem with this discrimination in organisations is the same as the problem with it in wider society: it is invidious, unfair and harmful, overlooking potential sources of value and expertise. It diminishes us all and condemns us to a world of ordinariness at best, and downright suspicion and wasted potential at worst. Yet still it persists.

Disasters such as the collapse of Barings Bank or the stench of corruption at Enron, Worldcom, Ahold and others are seen as examples of the perils of trusting human nature, when what is needed is more and more effective control and direction. For organisations and shareholders the wave of financial and accounting scandals in recent years has focused attention on the way that organisations are controlled. The possibility that respected firms might be guilty of accounting shenanigans depresses stock market prices, and the response designed to restore faith in standards of corporate governance has been to favour regulation.

Supranational bodies such as the European Union have steadily increased regulations in areas such as corporate governance, data protection and employment. During 2002, the United States introduced the Sarbanes-Oxley Act requiring CEOs to vouch formally for the accuracy of their firm's accounts. As journalist Lucy Kellaway comments:

Bureaucracy, after many years of decline, will be on the rise again. More regulation of companies, encouraged by the Sarbanes-Oxley Act in the United States, and other measures designed to clean up the corporate act will be the spur. The onus of proving that a company is whiter than white will bring huge time demands and a heavy paper trail with it.[3]

The paradox of audacity and the squandering of talent

Of course, some of these arguments are valid, but only up to a point. We have to find ways of not leaving ourselves vulnerable to malice, but *only* for malice. In killing the cancer of corruption and deceit we might end up killing the audacious patient. Or more prosaically, we may so inhibit the contribution that people individually and collectively make that we are squandering an organisation's most precious resource: its talent.

The problem is that everyone is trying to create the wrong sort of protective frame and influence in a limiting way the private strategies people have within each of the eight states. These 'policing' arrangements are trying to remove people so far from the 'dangerous edge' that they cannot harm anyone or in fact themselves. All this control inhibits the individuality of people, their freedom to be themselves, their opportunity to be wilful. By controlling people we repress their individuality; their ability to follow *and* break rules, to be team players *and* individuals, to be focused on goals *and* playfully experimental.

In uncertain times, as we saw from the volatility curve in Chapter 1, doing this is precisely the wrong response. Organisations rather need to develop confidence frames in themselves and in their people. Lacking this confidence can have consequences at the highest level. The Japanese are recognising the consequences of a restrictive culture. They have established the '*shippai-gaku*' or 'failure-ology' institute to try to work out how the once bright star of Japanese industry has stagnated for over a decade.

According to business writer Yotaro Hatamura:

> Japan has always been scared of the concept of failure. We didn't see it, we didn't watch for it and we didn't catch it. In the 1980s we felt that because we invented the 'total quality control' movement that was enough. It wasn't... The Japanese economic miracle was just us learning from other people's failures. The time has come to learn from our own.

The failure can be attributed to many causes, Hatamura says, but he specifically identified some cultural traits, one of which is the inability of individuals to make decisions.[4] Individual decision-making often requires not waiting for or even going against a cautious consensus.

So we are left with a paradox: How do we boost audacity to cope with volatility, without unacceptably increasing the potential for malice? The first question is: Can the paradox be resolved? The next is: Can we gain confidence in our people?

Can the paradox be resolved?

The greatest voice on this subject in recent years is that of the maverick Brazilian entrepreneur, Ricardo Semler. His company, Semco, was transformed from a struggling machine business into a profitable, innovative and exciting corporation in a few years, by actively recognising that work patterns were changing and that the full abilities of everyone in the organisation needed to be used. Semler's view is that people can participate in local and national democracy, contribute to the community, work as justices of the peace, raise children, express themselves through hobbies and other activities and have the knowledge and potential of the Internet at their fingertips – they are valuable and unique. However, when they go to work they are treated, en masse, as robots. He therefore set about finding ways to recognise, respect, reward and liberate his workers.

For Semler, the answer was not simply to graft empowerment on to an existing hierarchical structure. Instead, he took a more radical approach with workers empowered (if they wanted) to find out, discuss and help set the direction of the business, as well as implement it. For example, employees were able to decide the direction of the business, what their targets should be, salary levels and many other issues traditionally left to senior managers. In practice, they came to recognise where relevant expertise lay and to allow that knowledge to flourish. Furthermore, employees were paid not according to hierarchy or status, but the real value – meaning the scarcity – of what they did. All of this may seem like a socialist utopia, but it is in fact the polar opposite, placing great individual responsibility on Semco's employees. This responsibility was readily accepted. Individuals were given a much greater say in how their business fared, and a much greater control of their fate.

Semler recognises the difficulties inherent in this approach:

> At first it was hard for us. But with a great deal of commiseration and consultation, the shock of the 'rulelessness' began to subside, and our middle managers began to remove their armour plates. I like to tell them that a turtle

may live for hundreds of years because it is well protected by its shell, but it only moves forward when it sticks out its head.[5]

Semler's account of his day in an issue of *The Times*[6] would make an interesting comparison with that of many heavyweight corporate leaders.

8.45 am–1pm: Sit at my desk at home making a to-do list. After that, my day is unstructured. For twenty years I've had no watch… I do a lot of things by the sky: if it looks like rain I'll do more work. Passionate quick work doesn't become a chore. The Semco Foundation reflects that idea: employees are encouraged to gravitate to what ventures interest them.

1pm–2pm: Lunch with family.

2pm–6pm: Usually board meetings, though on three days a week I go horse riding in the mountains. Ideas for work come to me there. I spend at least an hour a day with my son.

6pm–2am: Two hours a day studying – surfing the net in an unstructured way. I never really finish work because something might interest me later in the day.

This from the Chairman of the fastest-growing service and manufacturing company in Latin America.

What do you get when you trust people to be audacious?

Despite huge publicity for Semler's approach, it has had relatively little impact upon the running of other global businesses. It seems to be more than a few steps too far for most global businesses. The destination looks unclear and the journey particularly tricky!

Does any of this matter? Put another way, isn't less audacity a fair price to pay for a secure, controlled organisation? At a time when many institutions, organisations and people are reeling from the effects of corporate accounting scandals affecting Worldcom, Arthur Andersen, Ahold and others, should we not avoid bold new management ideas in favour of disciplined command and control, perhaps seasoned with a little politically correct empowerment here and there?

The answer is no, for three reasons. First, because audacity and sound, ethical and effective management are not mutually exclusive. Moreover, it is precisely because people do not have an outlet for their natural impulse to be audacious that they can be seduced by the 'dark side', taking risky actions that are foolish and even illegal. They feel unable to create value the legal, audacious way, so they resort to financial trickery and worse, criminal acts of fraud. Second, as we have seen, risk-taking audacity is inherent in all of us – we need to be audacious to feel fulfilled and motivated – indirectly this will have consequences for an organisation in what McKinsey's has called the 'war for talent'.[7] That is how to recruit, retain, develop and deploy the best people.

Finally, as we have argued all through this book, organisations need people to be audacious if they are to walk the dangerous edge between success and failure, progress or complacency. We can be more specific about what audacity contributes to a business within a general willingness to face up to and personally deal with uncertainty and unpredictability. These last two points deserve further elucidation.

The people you want, want to be audacious

Case 1

I used to work for an organisation where people were neither valued nor fulfilled. The CEO's view was that as soon as anyone was trained they tended to leave the firm and work for a competitor. If they were given something in which they could take pride or feel fulfilled, perhaps becoming expert in a specific area, then he viewed that as an organisational weakness, making the firm vulnerable to that person leaving with their valuable knowledge. He had bitter experience of this, and his response was retrenchment: stop training or valuing people and instead work them hard. If they should choose to leave then bring on the next one. People were cannon fodder. Perhaps surprisingly, this autocratic approach had some success: people worked hard out of fear and pressure, and some good financial results were achieved, but it was not sustainable and it is hard to imagine that it ever could be. The business could not sustain its growth and in time the assets of the business – chiefly the customer database – were bought by a competitor.

Case 2

I worked at another company that valued the skills and experience I had developed, and although I was quite well paid it certainly wasn't top dollar. Some people did leave and they were wished well. Quite often they would be back within a year or two. This was the place to be. It was cutting edge, there was always something new going on. Part of its brand was to be different, to be bold. It was a friendly place even when things were not going so well. People wanted to join.

No one, not even the boss, was particularly motivated in Case 1, let alone fulfilled. What was lacking was one of the key pillars of audacity – motivational connection.

The war for talent

The McKinsey Report highlighted the growing shortage of supply in talented people as a worldwide phenomenon. A number of factors are accelerating this problem. Increasingly, small to medium-sized companies are capable of attracting good graduates. Also the changing nature of work pushed on by increasing globalisation requires increasing numbers of people who can entrepreneurially excel in disaggregated, multi-networked, cross-boundary businesses.

By 2015, McKinsey predicted that in the US there would be a 33 per cent increase in the demand for executives with an opposing 15 per cent reduction in supply.

When there is a shortage of supply then the seller dominates. Talent is mobile. So what do talented people want?

And this was the spooky bit when we came to write this book – talented people want to be audacious. That is our word not theirs, but the message is clear. The McKinsey Report highlighted the motivationally rich expectations of what talented people regard as a 'great job'. The number one factor – rated by 56 per cent of survey respondents as *essential* – was 'freedom and autonomy' (also known as *rebelliousness* and *self-oriented mastery* within the eight states of reversal theory). Another essential factor was a job with 'exciting challenges' (*playfulness*).

All in all, McKinsey identified six attributes of a great job, which we see as evidence that the needs in different motivational states can be met, particularly the states most associated with audacity (*playfulness*, *rebelliousness*, and *self-mastery*). These are the elbow and head room in which executives have the freedom to take responsibility, get things done and find new challenges to work on. They provide a clear link between activities and results (the *serious* state), something an executive can get his or her arms around and great colleagues (*sympathy*).

And *playfulness*? McKinsey quoted with approval David Vague, CEO of First USA:

> I aspire to create an enterprise where everyone's job consists of at least 80 per cent of the things they love doing.

The conclusion is simple and inescapable: to get the people that an organisation needs to thrive, you must have embarked upon the road to audacity.

Audacity delivers

It should now be clearer why people need to be audacious: so that they are more effective, fulfilled and motivated. Of course, this has a valuable, indirect benefit for employers and organisations that then reap the benefits of their motivated employees. However, audacious people also provide important, direct benefits for their organisations beyond the fact that as workers they are more motivated.

Ask any successful leader what qualities they feel are important, and whatever else they mention they will always say two things: first, an ability to get on with people, communicating, motivating and understanding others, and second, moral courage. This is the ability to lead from the front, take risks – even with one's personal credibility if necessary – and make difficult choices that work. The adjective courageous is impossible to separate from effective leadership – the former is an essential part of the latter. At some point, a leader will have to make a difficult choice or accept a reversal of fortune. One of the reasons why organisational control is so stifling and counterproductive is because it is an excuse to avoid courageous leadership. It can often be easier to hide behind procedures, policies or flawed interpretations of events, rather than trust people to take control and help them to succeed.

This is the antithesis of the management style at SABMiller, as CEO Graham Mackay made clear in our interviews, which form the basis of Chapter 10:

> To me it comes back to an independence of thought, a willingness to look at things fundamentally and say to yourself: 'what do you really think about it?' We need people who operate the business, willing to roll up their sleeves and get involved, get on with the job rather than hobnob with the gentry.

As part of their rapid expansion from large regional player to a huge global enterprise and the second biggest brewery in the world, SABMiller would send people out into new territories unsupported except for a credit card, a cell phone and an instruction to call home when they knew what they wanted. A manager there mentioned the new management recruit sent to work in a new market, who asked for a copy of the standard operating procedures. He was told to send head office a copy when he had written them.

Undoubtedly opportunities for this real pioneering management are drying up, as globalisation takes a hold even in the remotest parts of the world. However, Graham Mackay still wishes to retain the robust restlessness that made this success possible.

The creativity and personal responsibility implicit in audacious people can enable a more proactive positive approach to customers. Also, lest we forget, audacity can enable greater rewards in all states, in this case the *sympathy* state (another state that the report quoted above found under-utilised). The *sympathy* state is one central to genuine customer service.

The Ritz-Carlton hotel chain determined that its customers wanted a highly personalised service. This was important for the business to deliver so that it could differentiate itself from its competitors and provide a premium-value offer. The approach that Ritz-Carlton adopted won a prestigious Baldridge Award for quality and succeeded by emphasising several principles, all of which were underpinned by a blend of effective leadership and audacity. First, a vision of an efficient, personalised service was formed, and the individual commitment of employees to realising this vision and providing a quality service was then developed. Next, IT systems were standardised throughout the business and a culture developed that emphasised the need to capture and share useful information about each customer. The firm recognised the need to ensure that people, information and processes were working together to deliver a highly customised, attentive service.

Above all, each employee was encouraged to show initiative in meeting the needs of customers. Whereas control processes and procedures dominated much of the hotel industry, Ritz-Carlton believed that by empowering and trusting its people to act on their own initiative, it would be better able to meet the diverse needs of its customers. Whatever customers wanted – from theatre tickets to specific meals, newspapers or room configurations – Ritz-Carlton employees were taught never to say 'no', but to go out and make it happen. The result is a distinctive, high-quality brand that is able to justify a premium price and is recognised as different from its competitors.

The Ritz-Carlton approach is a stunning example of the power of *mass customisation* – the ability to deliver rapidly, efficiently and profitably a range of products and services satisfying individual customers.

Ritz-Carlton enables people to be audacious. It values people:

■ confident enough to experiment, trying out new approaches
■ whose thinking is characterised by creative open-mindedness, critical

analysis and unconventionality, enabling them to understand situations from their customers' perspective

■ who emphasise personal success, both formally and informally, controlling and mastering new commercial challenges.

... and is innovative

The word 'innovation' conjures up the image of a process that is spontaneous and unpredictable – even unmanageable. The innovation literature abounds with stories of serendipitous discoveries and independent-minded champions doggedly pursuing an idea until they hit the jackpot. Often – as the stories don't fail to stress – the inventors had to persist in the secret of their labs against the knowledge and will of senior colleagues. The archetypes of such innovators are Art Fry and Spence Silver, the 3M chemists who turned a poorly sticking adhesive into a billion-dollar blockbuster: Post-It Notes. In most of these stories, innovation proceeds from the labs or marketing outposts, not from the top of the organisation. In this situation, the role of management, in the view of former 3M CEO, Lewis Lehr, is 'to create a spirit of adventure and challenge'.

However, the role of senior managers in proactively developing innovation is often more significant and direct, and requires them to back the uncertain, sponsor the mould-breaking and allow in their people fresh, unconventional thinking. The commercial development of the credit card is an example. In 1958, a research group at the Bank of America, with the remit to develop potential new products, created the first credit card. This development was augmented later by seven bankers at Citibank who added the key features of credit cards, including merchant discounts, credit limits, terms and conditions.

This development *did not result from a market need*: it emerged because people within the banking business used their knowledge. This included their sense of the market and understanding of customers; information and forecasts about economic and social trends; experience with similar product ideas (such as instalment loans) and knowledge about new technological developments to devise a popular and practical service: the credit card. This heralded the beginning of innovation within the retail financial services industry, and this in turn led to such developments as ATMs and the growth of Internet banking.

There are several points to note about the credit card that distinguish it from the more famous serendipitous innovations such as the Post-It Note. First, senior management support was essential: they set up the unit, helped to develop its features and gave it the support needed to take root and grow. Indeed, in 1977 Citibank innovated in this sector again, this time with a marketing drive to increase its share of the lucrative market for credit cards in the USA. With a single *26 million-strong mailshot* it became, virtually overnight, the largest issuer of Visa and MasterCards in the world. This enabled Citibank to strengthen all of its activities, eventually becoming the world market leader in retail banking. This level of innovation required top-level support from the early stages of the process: creating the right conditions, enabling broad motivation and trusting its people with the information and resources they needed.

Summarising the direct benefits of audacity, we would suggest that if you are looking for the following you are in effect seeking a more audacious organisation.

Playful

- Are there situations when spontaneity is important and when opportunities need to be grasped?
- Is it important to be able to experiment – to feel like you *want* to experiment and try new things out, not all the time, but sometimes?
- Is being open-minded sometimes an asset, even essential?
- Is it important for people to immerse themselves in activities for extended periods of time without stress or even burn-out?
- Do you need exceptional productivity?

Rebellious

- Is it important to be able to break convention and demonstrate originality?
- Are independence and initiative important?
- Is an ability to handle conflict valuable?
- Are skills of critical analysis and evaluation necessary?
- Is differentiation a core strategic need?

Self-oriented (mastery)

Do you need people who:
- Are results-oriented and strive to succeed?
- Embrace responsibility?

- Are determined to learn, developing their own skills and effectiveness?
- Seek, control and master new challenges?
- Do you need less bureaucracy, less talking, *more* action?

The importance of *playfulness*, *rebelliousness* and *self-orientation* are not immediately apparent from the way that most organisations manage their people. This underlines the point made at the start of this chapter – that organisations are *afraid* of their employees – seem even more perverse. Instead of encouraging these motivational states, organisations can tend to emphasise their polar opposites: certainty not experimentation, process not spontaneity, control not openness. One consequence of this is a focus on the past, not the future. It is not that certainty, process and control are 'wrong', they are simply not enough on their own.

What does it take for an organisation to be audacious?

This chapter has focused upon the way that organisations stifle audacity: principally through not trusting their people, and expressing this lack of trust through control mechanisms that inhibit motivational life, particularly in the key aspects of playfulness, rebellion and self-mastery. We have examined how this affects organisations indirectly as audacity is something talented people want, and directly in that the business can achieve more by being more audacious.

The next chapter focuses on how an organisation can respond to this and enable a fuller expression of human motivation and potential. Key to this will be the leadership style collectively and individually of the whole business. What will be required is a leadership style that creates a climate in which people experience a broad range of motivational states in productive ways, balanced by a critical awareness of what is going on both personally and in the broader world.

The very big picture

At worst, there is something very sad and skewed about the way organisations, or at least the people who run them, view people. There is also something rather simplistic. You might start worrying about the people they hang around with given the narrow way that they see their employees and customers. Is it derived from a view of how successful business and economies must work, predicated upon self-interest and even greed? The most brutal expression of this narrow view of human nature in some of today's business models – little changed from that of Frederick Taylor – is that we all driven to contribute to an organisation or to society purely for the selfish rewards it offers.

According to the economist John Kay:[8]

> Some right-wing radicals go even further. It is a mistake to regard selfishness as a vice… private charity is thus the only proper mechanism for redistribution.

He goes on to argue, as we have done, that the world and motivation do not work like that:

> Real businesses designed on purely instrumental terms have proved, in the end, unsuccessful in the market economies' own terms. The piece rate systems of the factories were abandoned because they destroyed social relationships in the work place, provoked endless negotiation and conflict, and established a working environment in which no-one cared about the quality of the product.

He goes on to argue that:

> Economic motivations are complex, multi-faceted, and not necessarily consistent.

He highlights individuals like Warren Buffett, and his assertion that:

> It's not that I want money. It's the fun of making money and watching it grow.

To which we would add everyone we have spoken to in writing this book. No one who was successful in business cited money or self-interest in a narrow economic sense as the primary reason they worked. Not that money was an unimportant motive for some of them, but it was one of several, often contradictory perspectives.

The distinction between the man in the street and economic man or woman is a false one. Leaders of organisations need to look to their own families and friends and a wider circle of friends to understand their employees. Perhaps with this more realistic view they would not be so scared of them. Our understanding of how the economic world works and how people contribute needs to be founded upon their inconsistency and the richness of their needs and potential. Organisations should look around them: in an inconsistent world, it is not that we should trust some people and not others, but rather that we should have the understanding and aware-ness to know when to trust someone and when not.

We should acknowledge and celebrate diversity, placing audacity, rather than caution or distrust, at the heart of our relationships.

Notes

1 Carter, S., Desselles, M., Shelton, M. and Apter M.J. (2003) *The Apter Report on the Motivation of Managers 1*, Apter International, June. Copies can be obtained from Apter International, The Innovation Centre, Epinal Way, The University of Loughborough, England

2 Taylor, F. (1911) *The Principles of Scientific Management*, Harper & Row, New York. For a more recent analysis, see Taylor, F. (1948) *Scientific Management*, Harper & Row, New York

3 Kellaway, L. (2002) Boardroom Styles, The World in 2003, *The Economist*, November

4 Lewis, L. (2003) Japan Tries to Figure Out Where it Went Wrong, *The Times*, 7 April

5 Semler, R. (1994) *Maverick!*, Arrow, London

6 Collins, S. (2003) The Human Jungle, Interview with Ricardo Semler, *The Times*, 14 April

7 Chambers, E. et al. (1998) The War For Talent, *McKinsey Quarterly*, **3**

8 Kay, J. (2003) The Real Economy, *Prospect*

CHAPTER SEVEN

Leadership Matters

The reasonable man adapts himself to the world: the unreasonable one persists in trying to adapt the world to himself. Therefore, all progress depends on the unreasonable man. (George Bernard Shaw)

One of the primary, fundamental faults with American management is that over the years it has lost its zest for adventure, for taking risk, for doing something that no one has done before. (Harold Geneen)

The best leaders are apt to be found among those executives who have a strong component of unorthodoxy in their characters. (David Ogilvy)

Earlier in our careers, both of us worked at the Institute of Management in the UK. Although it was the largest professional body of managers in Europe its reputation and profile were somewhat mixed. Previously it had suffered from some quite serious problems that had caused significant wobbles to its viability. This situation had been stabilised largely through the careful and astute actions of John Robins, who had been recruited from a long and successful career as Finance Director with Marks & Spencer.

However, the Institute, then known as British Institute of Management, was very much a place that felt 'second division'. The moves and changes that were happening in the UK at the time involved it, but were certainly not led by it. The management team, with some notable exceptions, was a mixture of former managers from organisations for whom the Institute was a precursor to retirement, or they were much younger, more inexperienced people like ourselves.

To us it was great: a place in which you could gain experience, which at that stage in our careers would be hard to get elsewhere. However, it was not a place that you felt was forging dynamically ahead. Innovations and changes always seemed very hard to achieve. The structure of the

Institute meant that real decision-making often lay within an arcane structure of committees.

Then a new Director General (Chief Executive) was appointed.

The first reports were not encouraging. Roger Young was a city banker with what seemed an unhealthy appetite over things to do with Institute membership. With more curiosity than enthusiasm we all trooped into the library at head office to meet him. First impressions matched first reports. What we saw was a stereotypical banking executive: pinstripe suit and handkerchief flowing from his breast pocket. The only wrinkle to this vision was that he was wearing a badge with an L for Learner on it.

He introduced himself to us with a short speech. The L for Learner, he explained, was a present from one of his daughters. He was happy to wear it, he said, as he had much to learn and would need our help. He also promised to be very visible and present. I had only seen the previous Director General twice in the year I had been employed.

One thing he was absolutely sure about, he asserted, was that he was going to be the CEO – the chief excitement officer. And he meant it.

Working with Roger Young at the Institute was very different from what had gone before. People were held accountable for getting things done. Permission was not given; it was assumed that you already had it. Enthusiasm was offered and expected. Hierarchies were not emphasised. He held meetings with junior managers, asked them their views. He encouraged people to propose new ideas. He gave people responsibility. Within a few years the Institute had merged with a smaller body, established the largest management development qualification of its kind, launched in partnership with a publisher a remarkably successful series of management publications. The reports and views of the Institute were regularly featured on prime-time news programmes. The Institute started to take its innovative approaches overseas.

But Roger Young did not do all of this – or even much of it – himself. What he did was create the climate in which others, particularly the younger managers, had a clear vision of what they wanted to achieve: they felt able to do it. By acknowledging people's contribution, he made them feel confident.

Not everyone there at the time appreciated the approach, and no doubt mistakes were made – but we are not alone in remembering that period of time as a particularly productive and exciting one. So much so that nearly ten years later that group of managers still meet up twice a year in London.

What Roger Young seemed to understand was that something that increasingly is becoming apparent to those who would wish to enhance their leadership, and audacity, for that matter. It is that a great working climate is not a by-product of good leadership – it needs to be the core purpose of leadership.

This chapter argues that if organisations are looking for performance, then how people are motivated – meaning the internal climate in which they operate – is the primary lever with which an organisation can achieve this. This is not a careless assertion. It is something for which there is increasing evidence from academic institutions such as the Institute of Work Psychology at the University of Sheffield, professional bodies such as the Chartered Institute of Personnel and Development, and consultancies and research organisations such as Hay and Gallup. The implications of this are critical if organisations really want to achieve audacious levels of performance. Let's get this straight: we are arguing that getting the climate right is at least as important as process, strategy and structure. Get the right climate and you are a long way to creating the conditions in which these other factors can be successfully delivered. And what is the biggest single lever affecting the climate of an organisation? Leadership.

The need for leadership

If this is so, then there is a problem. Worldwide, there seems to be a growing sense of a lack of leaders and leadership. This is apparent at every level, from small teams to large organisations, even to nations and international institutions seeking to harmonise and protect life, liberty and commerce. A report by management consultancy firm McKinsey[1] put it this way:

> Rarely will the problem be poor strategy or the lack of a sound implementation plan. Most often, it lies in a mismatch between the leadership capacity available in an organisation and the scale of the task at hand. Most companies simply do not have the quality or quantity of leaders they need for the challenges they face.

The irony is that management magazines and journals have, for more than a decade, been celebrating the cult of the great leader. Look at any management textbook and the legions of omniscient, tough, clear-sighted field marshals appear. The supply-side problems of this would therefore be simple. Clone them or rather clone what they do. In one sense, that is what the ongoing search for leadership seeks to do.

Trying to capture and replicate what made Churchill great, or Jack Welch at GE, is a task that has engaged many professional and amateur researchers for decades. The outcome of this is usually a generic list of attributes that fails to capture the context and real circumstances in which the hero operated and conveniently ignores that for many, if not most of them, it all ended in tears. If you want to be mischievous, try to find a worthy magazine that did not celebrate and extol the achievements of the leaders of Enron or Worldcom. Many of yesterday's heroes are now spending an unhealthy amount of time with their lawyers.

Led astray: why traditional leadership ideas are failing

Notwithstanding this, the world craves strong leadership. The *Harvard Business Review*, itself not unblemished in the cult of leadership celebrity, has noted that 'a collective craving for symbols of reassuring leadership continues unabated'.[2]

It notes with approval the warnings of Rakesh Khuruna that:

> The charismatic CEO is a projection of people's yearnings for a knight in shining armour – rather than any attribute of an individual leader.

Quite frankly, it is time we grew up. Even if we could bottle what it takes to be the manager apparently embodied in the classic examples, then we are still going to have a leadership supply problem. It seems likely that we are looking for the wrong qualities, applying outdated notions of leadership to times and circumstances that are now very different in ways that we are struggling to comprehend. Undoubtedly, we are living through a period of change equal to, if not greater than, the industrial revolution – a time of change that fundamentally alters the way we organise ourselves, conduct business and interact. In these circumstances, what matters is the leadership spirit in all of us, not a quest for a mythical saviour.

Leadership is what matters, not simply leaders

There is a danger with the current paradigm that leaders are simply people in designated roles, yet the point is that organisations need leaders *everywhere* – particularly if they are to be audacious. The challenges of uncertainty and unpredictability mean that at any point in an organisation people may be called on to act as leaders, taking responsibility, using resources, creating change, supporting those who are struggling and insisting that expectations are met. Employees surveyed at Gore-Tex responded by saying that over 50 per cent had leadership responsibilities.

The breakthrough idea is that organisations misjudge the need: instead of looking for leaders, the search should instead be for leadership. The role of a leader is to ensure that leadership exists within the organisation. Leadership is a quality of the organisation as a whole, not just the domain of a few; and everyone plays their part.

We are all leaders now, and on occasions, all of us will need to be audacious.

Leaders need to work constantly to provide an environment in which those around them feel that all eight states can be met by their co-workers. They also need to create appropriate confidence frames and high levels of awareness. This is the *performance climate* in which audacity can be contemplated and sought out.

Developing audacity through leadership

Another brief moment of theory. Climate, as we see it, is the 'motivational proposition of an organisation'. This moves far beyond carrot and stick – goal and reward – approaches to motivation; it comes from addressing what is important to someone in each state. Organisations create environments in which certain states are encouraged and others discouraged. In an advertising agency, for example, it is often possible for people to occupy and be rewarded in the playful state, while in a bank, satisfaction is readily available while in a conforming state. Organisations often talk about wanting to change their 'culture'.

Culture, the manifestation of climate, results from the assumptions that people in the organisation make about how the world works, the organisation's symbols, routines and both formal and informal behaviours. If private strategies represent our motivational states in the way we deal with the world, then culture is an expression of organisations' climate. Following from this, if we talk about our motivational states having viable or non-viable private strategies, meaning effective and appropriate ways of gaining satisfaction, then it is possible to see that organisations can have viable or non-viable cultures, particularly in relation to audacity.

Now, culture is an arcane and complex phenomenon that is notoriously difficult to change. However, climate, within a structured reversal theory perspective with its direct link to individual experience, is much more manageable. The reasoning for this is that by addressing directly the varied motivational needs of individuals, leaders gain leverage on the culture, enabling it to change.

Investing time and effort to develop this type of working environment is likely to pay great dividends in the longer term, as organisations find that many of their other problems start to take care of themselves.

So how does an organisation achieve this, creating the conditions in which many (if not all) of its people feel committed to contributing to audacious leadership? There are two interlocking strategies:

■ First, enabling individual leaders to create microclimates in which there are the conditions to promote a rich motivational connection for those around them, plus the awareness and confidence to deliver an audacious contribution, then ...
■ Linking these microclimates through a 'leadership community' (an idea we will explore later) to develop the overall performance climate of the business. This enables a greater ability to respond innovatively and audaciously to volatile conditions.

Building microclimates

Imagine a leader who emphasises, through his or her actions, that individuals should feel empowered and responsible to take control of a situation, making sure that things happen. Initiatives are taken and work completed around them without the need for constant direction. Such a leader has created conditions of collective individualism in which individuals can take responsibility on behalf of others, and meet their needs for personal power within the self and mastery states.

The motivational state that we are in is a result of an interaction between our personal, shifting pattern of differing motivational states and the environment around us: the climate. This is an interaction between the way that we want to deal with the world at a particular time, and whether this is possible within a given situation. For example, we may be in the serious state, keen to achieve things that we find worthwhile, yet the organisation we work for and one's manager in particular offer little opportunity to do so. The vision and purpose of the organisation is unclear, and the manager just seems to go from day to day in a laid-back, reactive way. The manager may spend a great deal of time in states such as playful, sympathy and conforming, and as result, we are going to become very frustrated!

As we have argued, performance is largely triggered by the climate existing around a person, promoting or inhibiting the successful experiencing of different motivational states. While an organisation overall can be said to have a climate and a culture, it is also true that different leaders build their own climate around them.

Often, leaders create a narrow microclimate in which people can only be successful in one or two states, such as serious and conforming. What happens, however, when people in the team affected by the microclimate do not happen to be in those states? Inevitably, they feel frustrated; often feeling that an important part of who they are cannot be expressed. The result is that they cannot be themselves, withdrawing and reducing the contribution they make. In other words, they fail to fulfil their potential.

Leaders differ in the emphasis they give to underlying motivational states, creating different microclimates. Leadership style can be described as the way in which different leaders emphasise and make available each of the eight motivational states, and the values implicit in the microclimate around them. For example, if weather microclimates are characterised by various conditions, such as heavy snow, frequent fog or strong winds, then the performance climate around a leader can similarly be characterised by different conditions. The leader may create the microclimate condition of vision around them, meaning that people are clear on the purpose of what they are doing. They recognise the potential for purpose and achievement in the current situation, and therefore experience satisfaction in the serious state. Each of these conditions encourages different motivational states to be experienced successfully.

What's it like being around you? The eight microclimate conditions

We have found eight different conditions that exist in situations of successful leadership:

Vision

This is the condition in which people feel encouraged to look at activities in the long term, keeping in mind overall goals. Their orientation is to the future, seeing things in the broadest context and appreciating broad princi-ples. In a stronger form, it involves inspiring others with the goals to be achieved. It corresponds to the *serious* motivational style and to a basic value of *achievement*.

Enthusiasm

This condition emphasises enthusiasm for the task, making it interesting and even exciting. The leadership orientation is to get people energetically involved and engaged in their work. In one sense, and most obviously, it corresponds to the *playful* motivational state and to the basic value of *enjoyment*.

Structure

This is concerned with implementing roles, routines and procedures, making things run smoothly and increasing efficiency while reducing ambiguity and misunderstanding. It typically takes a bureaucratic form. It corresponds to the *conformist* motivational style and to the basic value of *fitting in*.

Constructive conflict

In this condition, the leader is concerned with encouraging innovation to bring about change in the organisation. It involves questioning assumptions and encouraging critical thinking that could lead to new and better ways of working. It is the 'grit in the oyster' leadership condition, which makes use of argument and creative conflict. It corresponds to the *rebellious* motivational style and to the basic value of *freedom*.

Collective individualism

This is the style in which the leader is concerned with developing a climate that encourages people to exercise power and authority. The states and values that are significant are *self* and *mastery*, the focus being on *personal power*. This can be individual power or control over processes, machines, tasks, or authority over people. The main benefit of establishing this condition is that individuals take responsibility on behalf of the whole, meeting their own needs and contributing to the group.

Shared resourcefulness

In this condition, the leader is concerned with fostering team co-operation and collaboration. The leader is focused on searching for what is best for the team as a whole, encouraging people to support each other through practical help, good communication, and in other ways such as mentoring and sharing of best practices. It can mean giving up things – information, time, resources, pet projects – to help others succeed.

If it is important for group effectiveness that individuals take power and responsibility for themselves, it is equally important that they feel motivated to add to the capability of others to deliver.

Shared resourcefulness corresponds to the *other-oriented* and *mastery* motivational states. The leader is encouraging personal power, creating conditions in which people feel motivated and empower others to succeed. 'Others' can mean individuals within a team or, as is increasingly important, other parts of the enterprise and beyond.

Trust and belonging

An essential part of enabling someone to feel able to take responsibility and contribute fully is a feeling of safety. In this condition, the leader is ensuring that his or her team is protected when necessary. Part of this assurance results from experiencing the confidence that comes from the leader emphasising the condition of collective individualism, but this is immeasurably strengthened by working in conditions where one feels liked, valued and supported. In these conditions, people feel able to contribute fully. A leader who does not establish conditions of trust and belonging, ignoring individuals' needs in the self and sympathy states, may allow politics and corrosive competition to prevail, with the consequence of poor performance and failure. A condition of trust and belonging is essential to the satisfactory experience of the states of *self* and *sympathy*.

Emotional commitment

Part of a leader's challenge in meeting individuals' self and sympathy needs is to encourage emotional support for others, enabling team members to meet their own needs for *other-oriented sympathy*. It is important to understand that this condition is different from shared resourcefulness, which is about building capability rather than emotional support. Many teams create incredibly tough environments that lack emotional commitment, and this makes it much harder for people to survive and thrive amid the bruising pressures of modern organisations. What is required is not simply coaching, but something subtler.

In profiling many managers, we have found big differences in the conditions that different managers establish and quite distinctive differences in their teams.[3] Even in the most rigid cultures and climates it appears that leaders can differ significantly in the microclimate they create.

If you want an audacious team, conditions of enthusiasm, constructive conflict and collective individualism will be particularly important. However, each condition has a part to play given that the absence of trust, support and emotional commitment can be destructive to audacious performance.

In building these conditions leaders need to themselves develop real awareness and confidence as climate builders – it is the basis of their right to be seen as leader. Climate-building requires of lot of quite subtle actions and a real ability to understand people as individuals.

Jean-Cyril Spinetta, the successful Chairman of Air France, has an interesting perspective on what it means to lead an organisation. First, value people. 'If you do not like people,' argues Spinetta,

> do another job. Understanding, motivating, mobilising and communicating with people are essential, and this is especially true in a service business such as an airline. The leader needs to uncover people's talents. The next quality is to reduce costs and be competitive, but also be sure that people understand the strategy. If people are unhappy or angry then the company suffers. Try to be transparent, clear and truthful. Even when it is difficult, above all when it is difficult.

Many management books would at this moment give you a neat checklist of '10 key things you should do to build climate'. Blithely following a 10-point list to try and build a new climate would be a superficial and futile response to a change in a complex arena. Each of us has to carve out our own approach, although we can learn much from watching others as role models.

Of course, most climate-building arises from our own behaviour. The way we personally act and the things we pay attention to are probably the most important factors behind an effective microclimate. Too many senior managers prefer not deal with this fact. Not only do they rarely make contact with their people, they indulge in behaviours based upon what turns out to be self-aggrandisement, which creates the climate that is almost guaranteed to hurt their business and the people in it. As we write this book the press is full of stories of senior executives taking exorbitant payouts as they exit companies that they have led to share collapse, massive redundancy and failure. We suspect the link is in part at least causal rather than correlational.

There is no way a climate that needs to sustain conditions of trust and emotional commitment can exist without leaders who act with integrity, with a genuine concern for others. And a lack of trust soon undermines conditions of collective individualism as people get wary about taking responsibility for things, and are uncertain of the basis upon which key decisions are being made. It is easy to see a domino effect on climate as a whole and thus on the way people are motivated.

Whatever our flaws, and no leader is without them, without basic levels of trust it is hard to see how a positive performance climate can be created with the inevitable benefits for performance. Audacity becomes almost inconceivable in an atmosphere where trust is absent, unless it is born of desperation.

A role model for climate-building?

For many people in England the name Nelson is synonymous with audacious heroic action. These are extracts from Christopher Hibbert's wonderful book *Nelson – A Personal History*,[4] which gives some indication of why Nelson should be held in the highest esteem as a builder of a performance climate.

He had never seen his sailors fight so bravely and with such bravery. Enveloped in smoke from their own guns firing with their muzzles inside the ports, deafened by the concussion, ignoring the hot blast of the enemy's muzzle flashes, they fought on even when wounded. One young man lost three fingers and later congratulated himself it wasn't his head; another told by an officer to go below to get a shattered toe seen to, said he needn't leave his post for a scratch and cut the toe off; a third sang 'Rule Britannia' all the way through while a surgeon amputated his arm.

The efficiency and bravery of his well-trained gun crews who could fire twice as fast as the enemy would compensate for any advantage in numbers which the enemy might have.

He had not the least pride of rank; he combined with that degree of dignity which a man of quality should have, the most engaging address. [Quoted by a contemporary.]

He said that his reception on joining the fleet caused the sweetest sensation in his life. 'The officers who came on board to welcome my return forgot my rank as Commander In Chief in the enthusiasm with which they greeted me. As soon as these emotions were past, I laid before them the plan I had previously arranged for attacking the enemy.'

It ran counter what he called, 'the old system of Fighting Instructions'. It entailed the risk of bringing down a potentially devastating fire upon his leading ships. 'I tell you what I think of it', he said 'it will surprise and confound the enemy. They won't know what I am about. When I explained (it) to them, it was like an electric shock, some shed tears, all approved – It was new – it was singular – it was simple!'

He seemed in excellent spirits, as he walked about, exchanging pleasantries with the sailors, speaking often of victory, as cheerful as he had been the night before when he had spoken airily of losing a leg in the forthcoming battle. [Again, a contemporary account.]

These men had grown not only to respect and admire him but regard him with affection. They knew that he would go out of his way to see that they were as well fed and clothed as could be arranged; that he would do his best to find occupations for them in the long boring hours of life at sea; that he would strive to see that good behaviour was rewarded. The timid, he never rebuked, prefer- ring to encourage them by demonstration and praise. He was solicitous for the welfare of the most lowly on board. He watched the subsequent careers of those who had served under him, 'with the closest attention, using his influence to advance them whenever it was in his power to do so'.

You can count off the motivational states that Nelson is trying to induce in these extracts. Yet this is a leader who certainly was no paragon. Else- where in the book Hibbert says of him:

He seemed a confirmed hypochondriac. 'I have been so ill since I have been here, that I was obliged to be carried to and from bed with the most excruci- ating tortures… I am physicked three times a day, drink the waters three times and bath every other night, besides not drinking the wine which I think the worst torture of all'.

And others of his contemporaries said of him:

He was devoured by vanity, weakness and folly, was strung with ribbons, medals, etc., yet pretended that he wished to avoid the honour and ceremonies he everywhere met with on the road.

He is vain and weak and therefore open to flattery and all its concomitants.

In spite of all appearances, (he) continued to strive to persuade the world and his own conscience that their relationship was as pure as it was ardent.

Apart from offering more evidence to support the reversal theory position that we are essentially inconsistent, these insights also suggest that there was deliberation in Nelson's approach, as well as a personal motivational connection that went beyond winning battles and collecting glory. His affection and commitment to the men he led was unarguable.

Time and again when you look at examples of audacious leadership you are struck by the fact that it is not just what the leader did that it is memorable, it is the way he or she created the conditions in which others did what they did that mattered.

Moreover, we should not assume that the leader is always responsible for directly generating all the conditions. A leader may well realise that certain conditions can best be developed by others and wisely makes sure they do not hinder this. A group may take on the responsibility for developing this climate without a designated leader – although this is likely to be quite a small group. It is for these reasons that it is important to distinguish between leaders and leadership

Sometimes a climate thus created can live on after the demise of the person who created it, such is the motivational connection they have managed to build. The influence of Mahatma Gandhi is an example of this. So was Robert Kennedy trying to build a vision of a new society, with the white population aware of the need for change and confident enough to let go of the prejudices of the past.

Mandela

It is not the case that climate-building leadership is some sort of soft, idealistic dream that may never come true. It requires toughness and a willingness to take a hard line, when needed. Probably few people in history can be said to have a greater positive impact upon the climate of a country than Nelson Mandela. He turned climate-setting into nation-building. His vision and strategy were inclusiveness and reconciliation. And yet he is and was tough, prepared from early in his life to see armed struggle as a necessary part of the fight against Apartheid.

Africa is a continent scarred by the effects of colonialism; the subsequent regime changes have often been marred by mass murder and other atrocities. Mandela managed to reach above this, recognising that the central purpose of his role as President of the Republic of South Africa was to avoid this happening. His personal acts of forgiveness to those who had abused and imprisoned him, knowingly theatrical in performance, created a powerful message to all the South African people.

He enabled others to be personally audacious and forgive their persecutors. And in doing so, had to move beyond the usual winner-takes-all approach of most changes of this scale, and find a way to in which people of all backgrounds and persuasions could find reward. For all the faults of modern South Africa there has not been the civil war and collapse of social order that many, perhaps the majority of thinking people, feared. Indeed, it is not unreasonable to argue that Mandela created a climate in which, against almost all the odds, the roots of a multiracial democracy could start to take hold.

The strongest seeds of this extraordinary vision, paradoxically, were formed during his 27 years of imprisonment. According to his friend and biographer, Anthony Sampson, his ordeal cut him off from mass audiences, the media and the trappings of power. In doing so he learned about

> human sensitivities and how to handle the fears and insecurities of others, including his African warders, (he was) stripped down to man-to-man leadership and the essentials of human relationships.[5]

Mandela was also sustained by the climate that was developed among his fellow prisoners. Collectively conditions of trust, sympathy and emotional commitment were developed, particularly with his close colleagues who reinforced his courage and his commitment to reconciliation.

No one could expect that leaders in business and other organisations could create a climate like Nelson Mandela, but there is no reason why any of us cannot attempt to develop an understanding of the paradoxes and inconsistencies that make us human. Through our own example we can try to create conditions where the motivational needs of those who lead are better met.

It may be that a leader needs to help people connect states to conditions and adapt their private strategies in each state so that they more readily gain satisfaction within a particular condition. For example:

- How I can connect my serious needs for achievement with the business within the vision? Achievement for me was making sure that internal processes ran smoothly, now the goal I am really committed to is increasing sales levels.
- To date other-oriented sympathy was a state I only experienced in relation to my family and closest friends. With the people I work with the way the condition of emotional commitment is expressed means I also perceive colleagues as included within these states.

■ Playfulness is something that is not for the workplace, work is serious –
until recently I never thought about work as something you might enjoy.

Helping people to make these connections is a subtle art and subject to
ongoing research. Leaders do it in a number of ways: reframing by
painting a familiar scene in different ways to highlight new aspects of it,
through persuasion and influence, through comparisons and so forth.

Fortunately, these connections can and often do occur more spontaneously, usually as the result of an act or action that is seen as hugely
symbolic. Mandela coming on to the pitch at the end of the 1995 Rugby
Football World Cup final, a game that had been exclusively seen as the
preserve of white people, wearing the Springbok shirt of the winning
South African team, instantly caused thousands of white people to feel
connected to the new order in many different motivational ways.

The demon seen

Earlier we talked about the need for a rich motivational connection for
audacity to be sustained by awareness and confidence if it is to lead to
successful behaviour.

You might argue that building climate is really a political art. It is a
way of manipulating people's feelings so that they don't really acknowledge current reality. This is the devious art of spin doctoring and the
political search for the feel-good factor thus sustains political power and
control. If leadership was only about providing 'the mood music' to keep
everyone happy, then this is hardly a lever for vibrant, audacious activity
that delivers results. Organisational leadership would be like the Pied
Piper of Hamelin whistling his followers to disaster. In climbing, audacity
without awareness would be suicidal; it is no less dramatic in business.
The problem is that often in raising awareness we are inevitably going to
concentrate on consequences and future outcomes. This places us firmly
in the serious state with its associated experience of anxiety when uncertainty abounds.

This is why awareness is the most difficult factor of all. The inclination
of many people to avoid reality, to pretend something is not happening, is
something that many would-be leaders collude with. It takes real toughness to resist this. This is why Churchill was a great wartime leader:
time and again he was prepared to confront the people with the reality of
their situation:

I would say to the House, as I said to those who have joined this Government, that I have nothing to offer but blood, toil, tears and sweat. We have before us an ordeal of the most grievous kind... You ask, what is our policy? I will say it is to wage war, by sea, land and air, with all our might and with all the strength that God can give us: to wage war against a monstrous tyranny, never surpassed in the dark, lamentable catalogue of human crime. That is our policy. You ask, what is our aim? I can answer, in one word: It is victory, victory at all costs, victory in spite of all terror, victory, however long and hard the road may be; for without victory there is no survival.[6]

The climate he created swept away the policy of capitulation strongly held by many of his senior colleagues.

Raising and maintaining awareness of reality is central to successful leadership. This awareness, as we saw earlier, includes personal awareness, awareness of the immediate circumstances and awareness of the broader situation. It can also include being honest and making people aware of what is *not* known.

Keeping people aware of what is going on is a tough one. There is huge temptation to hide bad news from staff, colleagues, bosses and even oneself. In doing this we are taking responsibility away from people. For example, if I don't see the situation I can't be expected to respond appropriately, therefore my best course of action is to do nothing.

An audacious leader is unafraid of building awareness personally and in others. In doing so they may well be *lessening* the anxiety. The demon seen is usually smaller than the demon imagined. Audacious leaders will also seek to raise *self*-awareness in others through their own actions as role models, through skilful questioning and appropriate feedback.

Captain Mainwaring and Private Fraser

The trick for a leader who wants to develop audacity is to maintain awareness and confidence. Without confidence there will never be a protective frame that enables people to be in the playful state. (Remember, audacity does not require that you are always in the playful state, but the rewards would be a bit thin if you were never in this state and stress and burn-out would be a real possibility.) On the other hand, feeling confident all the time without any real awareness of what is really going on would be highly delusional.

Dad's Army was a grand old BBC series set in World War II among a group of part-time soldiers, those too old, young or decrepit to be called up for the regular army. One of the principal characters was Private Fraser, the local undertaker, who was a Scot with a deep, emotionally wrought brand of pessimism. Faced with any misfortune he would roll his eyes and his 'r's, and exclaim to his commanding officer: 'We're doomed, Captain Mainwaring; we're all dooooomed!'

Captain Mainwaring was his leader, the pompous local bank manager, who was indefatigably confident in his own abilities, authority and position, without a shred of evidence to sustain him in this belief.

These represent two archetypical positions on dealing with audacity. A successful leader knows to deal with a Mainwaring-type by a judicious raising of awareness, and he or she also needs to be able to deal with their Private Frasers. The trick is to put Private Fraser back in control as much as possible.

The first challenge is: How do I build Fraser's confidence without dulling his awareness? The answer is encouraging his awareness to be non-judgemental, as we discussed in Chapter 5. By focusing on the facts of what is going on rather than the imagined consequences, we keep focused on the things we might do something about.

This leads neatly into how a leader focuses on building confidence. The secret, as we have seen, is to make the world small and manageable, and use the three control levers: situation, contribution and reaction. What is needed is for people to be able to define where and how they can exert the maximum amount of control. A leader will show if and how people can change the situation, where they need to be involved and where they have choices. Sometimes people feel they control the situation if they know more about it and what the odds are.

A leader can make explicit the choices others have about *how* they contribute. People can feel more in control through the timely delivery of appropriate development. Finally, a leader can help others feel more in control by helping them reframe a particular situation so that they feel more in control of it.

For example, a clever reframing came from a colleague who was helping several managers who were only a year or two from retirement and were faced with a level of change that, quite frankly, they did not have the heart or the stomach for. Working with them, she helped them see that this was not a situation in which they would succeed or fail, but one in which they had the choice and opportunity to coach others to help them deliver the change. This ability to reframe is a very powerful part of a leader's armoury.

Again, the power of role-modelling either by the leader or someone else can emphasise that control is available and that this is something that people can deal with.

Leadership communities

Looking back, what we experienced at the Institute of Management was what I have since come to term a 'Leadership Community'. What developed was a group of people who were prepared to support each other, to cross formal boundaries to provide help and resources, to create informal teams to take advantage of opportunities and threats. Increasingly, I have to recognise that such communities exist within many of the most successful organisations, particularly those that can audaciously adapt to change. HSBC, which transformed itself from a regional bank in South-East Asia to become one of the most powerful financial institutions in the world, deliberately created a cohort of International Officers (now called International Managers). This group was network-bound by strong ties and loyalty and could quickly be mobilised to manage mergers and acquisitions, entry into new territories and markets, implementation of new systems. South African managers within SABMiller seem to have established the same cohesion more informally. Jack Welch at GE went out of his way to create the spirit of the locker room within that organisation. Crucially, a community is not just a fancy name for a team.

If you think of the communities that you belong to, it is unlikely that you know everyone within them. Yet it is also likely that you feel a sense of allegiance to these strangers and that you share something. Even possibly that you could expect something from them. There are common stories and legends, shared heroes. Often they are characterised at least metaphorically by the 'happy band and its journeys' discussed earlier in the book. The narrative of communities often describes the hard journey, the struggles overcome, whether that be the great migration west in the US, those that launched the killer new product or established a new record low score at the golf club.

Communities are some of the most powerful and enduring of human structures. If you regard churches or the great world religions as communities then we are dealing with something that far outlasts any modern enterprise and regularly provides the context for extraordinarily audacious behaviour.

What communities do practically is to provide a flexible network through which information can be communicated rapidly, responses to opportunities and threats rapidly mobilised and resources allocated and shared. Often there is a self-forming quality to communities enabling smaller groups to form spontaneously. Often, too, membership offers rights of access and support that transcend formal hierarchies and positions. The advantages of this to an organisation are enormous as potentially structures can be formed and broken up to meet the changing demands of the marketplace.

What communities do emotionally is probably even more critical. Individuals can often sense that the power of the community is at their disposal, creating the condition of collective individualism in which people really feel able to set ambitious strategies for their self and mastery needs.

They make the bigger stuff manageable.

Often, communities are formed to 'stand against' something, creating the conditions of constructive conflict in which new and radical ideas can receive a real boost. Obviously healthy communities are the source of support and the place we find our friends.

It would be naive to claim that communities are not without their problems. In an organisation, there is always the danger of introspection, group-think and exclusivity, and organisations will need to work hard to overcome them. However, they are both an enormous source of continuity and, if mobilised, a massive lever for change.

Can these leadership communities be built? Building leadership communities requires replicating and accelerating the conditions through which they develop naturally. This requires:

- Creating a powerful shared experience.
- Modelling ways in which the community works together across boundaries.
- Heightening awareness of how community members can contribute and where this is different from current work contribution.
- Building confidence in this new way of working within the community.
- Ensuring early success in the real world for the community.

An organisation that audaciously initiated a project to do this is Boots Manufacturing in the UK.

Developing a performance climate through a leadership community

Boots Manufacturing (BM) is part of Boots plc, the long-established British retail and pharmacy chain. BM produces over-the-counter medicines as well as own-brand cosmetic and beauty products such as shampoos and bath products. The competitiveness of BM had, over many years, become obscured and eroded by its heavy reliance on one 'internal' customer, Boots the Chemist, the high-profile retail arm of the business. Manufacturing processes in BM had not kept pace with competitors or developments in other industries, with the result that costs were high, margins small and defect rates unacceptable. In this situation, BM decided against greater control in favour of greater *focus*. The management took considerable time and effort explaining to all of its employees the bare facts – that things needed to improve and that everyone was needed to play their part. Having set the scene and painted two alternative visions of the future, good and bad, it then explained where improvements and business salvation would come from: greater focus on customers, and greater use of lean manufacturing techniques. Lean manufacturing *requires* a mindset that makes innovation and improvement an essential part of everyone's job. It emphasises personal responsibility and the problems and opportunities are addressed cross-functionally.

To underpin these changes it was realised that the performance climate of the business had to be radically changed. People could no longer think and do what they always did. Partly because of its background in pharmaceuticals – Boots had once been significantly involved in R&D as well as manufacture of prescription drugs – this was a safe, conservative organisation driven by function and the careful construction of boundaries. It was a place that emphasised conformity and limited decision-making. It was also a 'paternalistic' organisation that looked after its employees – and it was going to have to lose headcount.

This was a very painful moment for the business. Losing people in the numbers required directly challenged its perception that it should 'care for' its people.

It was in the heat and the melting pot of these changes that the company audaciously decided to run its Chamonix programme, since described by Head of Manufacturing, Adrian Potter, as 'a watershed in the way we develop people'.[7]

> The executive knew that we were going to have to get the business back up and moving again [said Andrew Kerry, Organisational Development Manager at BM]. And yes, it was partly about morale. But it was also about bringing something new to the way people worked.

It was audacious. It broke the assumptions about when you should develop people. The Managing Director, John Watson, recognised that organisations needed to develop leaders and others for the change envisaged, not, as many organisations do, after the change. Despite the obvious perceptions of running the programme in such circumstances he understood its criticality and was prepared to back it.

The Chamonix programme took in tranches of about 20 managers at a time (150 in all), to a five-day leadership programme set in Chamonix in the French Alps.

Everything about the programme was designed to enable all of these managers to gain awareness and confidence in a completely new way of working and establish a leadership community which would support and promote the major strategic changes now under way within the business. Everything about the programme was also designed to signal that changes were happening. Hence the French Alps – chosen not because it was cheaper than running a similar programme in the UK (which it was), but to provide the compelling common experience from which a community can spring into existence. Although it was not an outward-bound programme, the outdoors was used where appropriate to mirror key factors in the workplace environment. The programme presented the participants with an intriguing integrated set of challenges that modelled the tasks and the process and leadership demands of the new way of working. One of the challenges ensured that each programme had to deal with and collaborate with preceding and subsequent programmes. Critically, no organisational structure was given to the group, nor was it possible for them to divide purely into discrete teams to tackle each challenge. Instead, the cohorts had to explore a more flexible way of working and make it efficient and effective. They also needed to establish a performance climate that maximised everyone's contribution.

Participants were helped to develop strategies to deal with their own 'dangerous edges' that might stand in the way of their performance.

The challenges were also about responding to risk and shaking assumptions of what was possible, a vital component of Boots' leadership plan. The company wanted its leaders to take responsibility for their actions rather than hide in the 'culture of permission' that had previously pervaded. Andrew Kerry highlighted the impact of this programme on the culture of the organisation:

> You can change people's behaviour. The expression of a culture is primarily through the way people behave. If you start to change the way people behave with one another then you start to change other things too.

Outputs from the programme linked directly and immediately back into the workplace strategic agenda.

Was a leadership community built? Yes, and many things changed. But as with all communities, individuals place themselves at different degrees within it. Perhaps a measure of its success is that managers who fail to maintain the 'Chamonix mindset' and fall back into less responsible, less audacious ways, are easily recognised and are identified by their colleagues as getting in the way. At the time of writing, the organisation is now much stronger and business performance is improving. Tough decisions have been made as the organisation shakes itself from being a traditional employer to a competitive, effective and lean business. The challenge remains, however, to move this approach as far and as fast as possible.

The formula

In writing this chapter, it may seem that we are merging ideas about leading for high performance with leading for audacity. That is because we believe that high performance absolutely hinges upon enabling audacious behaviour. So, the formula for developing the two is the same. The formula is therefore simple but subtle. Leaders looking for audacity create the conditions in which all eight motivational states can be met. One of the most powerful consequences of this is that it will promote the self-mastery motivated behaviour of personal responsibility, as well as other key behaviour driven by playfulness and rebellion. To drive this forward a leader will need to maintain high levels of awareness and confidence in those around him or her. This largely centres upon building the levers of control, making the world as small and manageable as possible.

Companies that want to be audacious will promote this by encouraging the growth of 'leadership communities' that can potentially develop the climate at an organisational level. One of the opportunities this may deliver is for the organisation to start to interact with its customer base more audaciously.

Notes

1　Hsieh, T.-Y .and Barton, D. (1995) Young Lions, High Priests, and Old Warriors, *McKinsey Quarterly*, 2
2　Editors (2003) The 2003 HBR List: Breakthrough Ideas for Tomorrow's Business Agenda, *Harvard Business Review*
3　Ongoing research at Apter International on climate-setting by managers. Using the Apter Leadership Profile, we are measuring both the climate that managers are intending to set and that experienced by their teams
4　Hibbert, C. (1995) *Nelson – A Personal History*, Penguin, London
5　Sampson, A. (2000) *Mandela – The Authorised Biography*, HarperCollins, London
6　Quoted in Jenkins, R. (2001) *Churchill*, Macmillan, London
7　For further details of this case see Blau, R. (2002) Radical Retreat, *People Management*, 2 May. Whereas most courses start with a trainer marching into a classroom and asking everyone to introduce themselves, Boots' leadership programme started in a field knee-deep in snow – talking about the business and the mountains, and the mindset that achievement in both had in common. Every day began with a walk, and one day was spent abseiling down an ice wall and traversing a glacier

CHAPTER EIGHT

Of Wildebeest, Buffalo and Bison

So, who should line up in the parade of audacious businesses? Until recently, the usual suspects would have been the bright young things of the technology industries, or perhaps some Internet business that had stolen all the headlines. Unfortunately, current data would be difficult – such businesses have either gone bust or are in hiding. Audacious they may have been – but successful? Only for a moment, and despite their audacity, rarely because of it. Of course, some businesses in these sectors will be successful again, and undoubtedly some of these can be fairly classed as audacious. However, in looking for role models it is useful to avoid always equating brilliant product innovation with audacity. Audacity, as we have tried to picture it, is a richer and more complex phenomenon.

HSBC and SABMiller are two interesting examples of the way the 'audacity factor' can work in two very traditional sectors: banking and brewing. There are interesting parallels between them. Fifteen years ago both were large regional players not really represented in the North American and European markets. Now, through organic growth and bold acquisition, they are very prominent members of the FTSE 100 and Dow Jones Index; both hold arguably a number two position globally in their markets, and both have made major acquisitions of major US brands – Household Finance and Miller respectively.

We suspect that the word 'audacious' would not be one that sat comfortably with either firm or with their industry commentators. Indeed, the *Wall Street Journal*[1] has described HSBC as boring, commenting on 'The dull but probe-free and steadily profitable conservatism of HSBC.'

Yet, in many ways their separate journeys demonstrate how organisations in 'old economy' industries can distinguish themselves by idiosyncratic wilfulness.

It seems that both firms are relative outsiders to the institutional financial worlds, which comment on and analyse them. Perhaps it is their origins outside Europe, the US or Japan that makes them interestingly unprepared to do what is expected of them by fashion, fad or fancy.

About SABMiller

- In a little over five years, this venerable South African conglomerate, first established in 1895, has risen to become one of the leading brewing companies worldwide. SABMiller plc is the world's leading brewer in developing markets and the second largest by volume, with 118 breweries in 24 countries.
- In the late 1980s, South African Breweries was that country's largest consumer group, accounting for 13 cents in every rand that was spent by consumers.
- In 1994, the year of the first fully democratic election in South Africa, resulting in a five-year Government of National Unity, SAB was invited to revitalise the beer industry in Tanzania, a joint venture with that country's government. It was also invited to re-enter the beer markets of Zambia, Mozambique and, later, Angola. Joint control of the second largest brewery in the People's Republic of China was negotiated with the government. Its achievements were recognised in 1995, when President Nelson Mandela opened SAB's Centenary Centre in the cultural precinct of Johannesburg.
- In 1997, recognising the need to enhance long-term shareholder value, SAB returned to its core beverage business, locally and internationally, selling off or closing non-core operations. SAB's commitment to social responsibility was affirmed in 1998 when it published its first corporate citizenship review. By 2001, turnover from SAB's international operations accounted for 42 per cent of group turnover, a remarkable achievement in a relatively short period. In 2002, SAB plc acquired 100 per cent of Miller Brewing Company, the second largest brewery in the United States by volume, and changed its name to SABMiller plc. This acquisition made SABMiller the second largest brewer by volume in the world.

And all this from a business sheltered away in a country that for much of the twentieth century was isolated, poorly run and ostracised.

About HSBC

HSBC's history is no less rich and lengthy.

The Hongkong and Shanghai Banking Corporation was established in 1865 to finance the growing trade between China and Europe. Since then, it has coped with tectonic shifts in the political, economic and social organisation of its main markets. It has endured two world wars, including the occupation of Hong Kong by the Japanese and the closure of many of its operations; the Cultural Revolution of the 1960s in China and the return of Hong Kong to China in 1997. Strategically, HSBC has sought to balance growth both in developed economies and in emerging markets. Along with the 1992 acquisition of the UK's Midland Bank (itself formerly one of the largest banks in the world) it created a new company, HSBC Holdings. This firm, located in London and quoted on the Hong Kong and London stock exchanges, consolidated its ownership of a range of businesses worldwide.

Growth continued through the 1990s to include banks in Brazil and Argentina, and the purchase in 1999 of Republic New York Corporation and Safra Holdings SA. This reinforced the group's presence in the United States, Switzerland and Luxembourg. Moving into Europe in a more substantial way was achieved by the purchase of CCF (Crédit Commercial de France), a major French bank. In 2002 the group completed the acquisition of Grupo Financiero Bital S.A. de C.V. in Mexico. In 2003, HSBC finalised its acquisition of Household International, Inc., a leading US consumer finance company with 53 million customers and over 1,300 branches in 45 states.

To the uninformed, these industries may appear unfashionable, but they certainly seem able to do interesting things! What are the key ingredients of their success?

Interesting and exceptional organisations

Wilfulness

The first of these is an ability to avoid following the herd.

When we interviewed Graham Mackay, SABMiller's chief executive, he was cautious about the word audacity and in particular the idea of wilfulness. However, a real feature of the SAB story is the fact that they chose not to take the easy path or the well-trodden route. Mackay commented ruefully about the pressure from commentators and analysts when the business first located to London to do what at the time seemed essential to future business success. The hype was intense.

I was constantly being asked 'what is your Internet strategy?' My thinking was 'I don't have a strategy for janitorial services, why have I got to have an Internet strategy?' But you were a derelict Chief Executive if you didn't have one. Audacity meant saying 'hold on, how is anyone going to make money out of all this?'[2]

HSBC showed a similar independence of view when they refused to pay bonuses to their equities and corporate finance staff after that part of the bank had made a loss of $112 million. There were outraged tantrums as the comfortable expectations of this well-heeled part of the financial services community were turned upside down.

Awareness

Graham Mackay recognised that the position of South African Breweries in the Apartheid era, despite the many manifest problems, was very comfortable from a business point of view. Paradoxically, its isolation made companies feel very protected: there were tariff barriers, accountancy controls and a reluctance of foreign competition to get involved in what was perceived as a 'ticking time bomb'.

This comfortable situation meant that SAB, at that time a conglomerate encompassing a whole range of activities, made good profits and enjoyed a surfeit of the best of South African managers.

However, Mackay and a few others were aware that this situation was marred by the fact that the economy was not really going anywhere, and that South Africa was drifting away from the community of nations. This awareness was heightened by the fact that they were distanced from the ruling elite. During the 1980s and 1990s the business had never been a favourite of the Apartheid regime despite its economic significance, as the leaders of the government had personally invested in the wine industry and were not keen on brewing. Moreover, according to Mackay, SAB customers

> were black people who were disenfranchised and were not part of the comfortable commercial round ... the underlying realities of South African society were much more in our faces than they were of most business managers in South Africa. We were a huge consumer company and our consumers were, by and large, black.

Their awareness of these issues led the business to take a number of challenging initiatives. One was to divest itself of all its non-brewing businesses and concentrate on developing a world-class brewing operation with increasing focus on developing an international profile – a process that obviously accelerated after the fall of Apartheid.

Another challenging initiative was a decision to develop world-class manufacturing (WCM) within South African Breweries – the drive for which showed astonishing confidence and awareness of the issues involved. After years of Apartheid, production line staff were poorly educated and lacked the technical and team working skills required by WCM. After a relatively short pilot project, a bold implementation plan was developed which included deploying temporary staff in areas being converted to WCM so that selected employees could be retrained on a full-time basis away from the workplace. Two further years of coaching and support were provided during which employees were encouraged to demonstrate that the necessary skills and competencies were being acquired.

The business also led many organisations in South Africa in developing non-white staff into supervisory and managerial positions, with a continued, sustained commitment that demonstrates a lack of self-congratulation and a willingness to be self-critical and challenging.

This level of awareness includes a refreshing acknowledgement that the vagaries of luck and chance have played in its direction. Certainly, some of SAB's success can be put down to good fortune: happenstance meant that the collapse of Apartheid coincided with the opening up of overseas markets. If the developing markets in China, Latin America and Central Europe had opened up ten years earlier, SAB would have been excluded as a firm from an ostracised country with an Apartheid regime. As luck would have it, history favoured SAB. Mackay uses this to promote a robust awareness in the firm, and a need to avoid complacency, embracing constant change and continuous improvement.

South African Breweries reinvented itself in its journey from a sprawling regional conglomerate to global giant, by recognising both the reality of its position and the assets it enjoys, including a strong cash position and real in-depth management talent.

This awareness results in an early recognition of, and reaction to, emerging events, with a strong organisational response. Sir John Bond, Chairman of HSBC, believes this is vital:

> Our aim is to be prepared for a wider range of eventualities – ideally, to be able to interpret as normal human affairs what others see as crises.

Confidence and the protective frame

'As South Africans, we weren't really frightened of emerging markets compared to the things that we were going through at home', comments

Mackay, who views disadvantages as positive factors. Difficult trading and
environmental conditions bred a hardy group of managers: ingenious, flexible, determined and prepared not to follow convention. This was highlighted by their bold move into developing economies, even before these
markets had strengthened and shown promise. Having built SAB in their
domestic market they were now keen to travel and prove themselves on a
wider stage. As an example of this, SAB entered markets that at that time
(the early and mid-1990s) were unfashionable, in Latin America, China
and Central Europe. Although these developing economies represent
attractive growth markets now, the fact that SAB had a culture of taking on
challenges meant that it could go there first and achieve considerable
success: enough to make it profitable and to encourage others to follow. At
times, SAB's audacity meant taking the course that it knew and preferred,
even if this meant seeming to stand against the tide and waiting for it to
change. Comments Graham Mackay,

> To me, it comes back to independence of thought, a willingness to look at
> things fundamentally and say to yourself, what do you really think about this?
> Where does that come from? What are the fundamental underlying facts, trends
> or tendencies?

Above all, SABMiller possesses a bold sense of confident mastery. SAB
managers run their business like Australians play cricket: focused, confident and delighting in risk.

Similarly, HSBC has had the confidence and management talent to
embrace banks in emerging markets that at times have been on the verge
of collapse. Throughout its history it has also been prepared to open
banking facilities in regions and countries where such facilities don't
exist – it continues to operate banking in some of the most difficult operating environments in the world. The fact it does do so profitably builds
and maintains a continuing confidence that it can succeed.

Motivational connection and leadership

HSBC and SABMiller are led by people, Sir John Bond and Graham
Mackay respectively, who have not courted the publicity and personality
cults of many of their contemporaries. John Bond goes to work on the
London Underground, travels economy on many short-haul flights and in
2001 received total compensation of $2.8 million. A large sum, but a frac-
tion of the $26.7 million paid by a key competitor to its chairman,
excluding stock options, according to filings with the Securities and

Exchange Commission. Sir John's manner and behaviour emphasise a key value of the group: that no individual's interest should be put ahead of that of the group as a whole.

Graham Mackay believes that SABMiller's success is certainly not the result of a single leader. However, it is very likely that given the circumstances prevailing at the time, a more cautious vision could have settled for the business sitting tight and taking its profits. It was Mackay who had the vision to prepare South African Breweries to become a world-class business and for this to happen, things had to change.

Both Bond and Mackay have striven to create a climate in which they feel able to respond to new challenges. Both continually emphasise the need for change, seeking out and countering complacency. Both create and make real a clear vision of what is important. Both lead businesses where personal integrity and responsibility are emphasised. Indeed, values are key in both businesses and imbue their actions and strategy. HSBC has, according to the *Wall Street Journal*, benefited from its refusal to become involved in the accounting shenanigans and 'questionable practices' that have tarnished the industry as a whole.

An emphasis on values characterises both organisations; this is emphasised and driven by both leaders and has created the potential for motivational connection that is deep and strong. These are organisations of which, in different ways and across many cultures, employees can feel justly proud.

Both organisations have benefited from the fact their history has given them leadership communities that have enabled this rapid growth to occur and be managed. HSBC highlights this approach with its cadre of International Managers. By emphasising management development and the nurturing of talent, SAB had been able to accrue during the Apartheid era a closely knit pool of managers who would be able, when the time was right, to take on tough international challenges. Their skills were honed for whatever may occur, whether it was turning round ailing existing business or starting new ones in environments in which the principles of good business were less well developed.

These leadership communities create and endorse a management style that seems to naturally reflect many of the motivational states. Each business is conforming in certain respects, clearly wanting to compete and become an integral part of its markets. However, rebelliousness is evident in the robust, frontier style that its managers bring to building brands and doing business. SABMiller managers are ambitious for themselves – keen to travel and build careers outside South Africa – but they are also genuinely focused on developing their employees and treating people with integrity because this is seen as benefiting the business. Like the International Managers at HSBC, the community also fosters strong personal relationships.

Both businesses now face the challenge that as a result of their rapid growth established leadership communities are now in danger of being spread too thin. Furthermore, having what may be perceived as an elite group so closely identified with such a homogeneous background is not appropriate for a global business. Both organisations will face the challenge over the next few years of sustaining and replicating the integration and identity that such groups brought to the business, and maintaining the motivational proposition that has created their tough independence of spirit.

In responding to the challenges of growing local talent and developing internationally effective managers who do not necessarily come from South Africa, Graham Mackay recognises that this will change the company and culture. Moreover, the company, having come through a massive growth phase, is seen by Mackay as being ready for a fresh injection of people with different attitudes. However, above all he wants to retain managers' confidence and restlessness.

SABMiller's restlessness is shown by its desire for constant improvement. This is what Mackay means by needing to stay restless: anticipating challenges and opportunities. As CEO, Graham Mackay believes it is this attitude that has sustained the business and kept it going – change followed change because of a restless climate where people wanted to do better, take on more challenges, be first and go further.

Keeping out the herd

Neither of these businesses is any sense perfect – I suspect that not being given to self-congratulation, they would probably agree. In both their climates and style, they can inhibit certain motivational states that may create blind spots in the way they deal with the world. Also, past achievement is no guarantee of future success, and we are conscious that we have seen and commented on the best of them. Notwithstanding this, their adherence to strong values, their awareness, confidence and independence of spirit make a powerful argument for regarding them as audacious businesses.

Notes

1   Portanger, E. (2002) Thrifty, Cautious Institution Weathers The Hard Times by Avoiding Hot Trends, *Wall Street Journal*, 28 October
2   All SAB quotations from an interview with Graham Mackay, conducted by Steve Carter in February 2003

CHAPTER NINE

Dancing with Customers

Desperately conforming incorporated

Is your best friend a corporation? Do you long for 6 pm, when you know that those nice telesales people will start calling your home? Do you shout 'yippee!' when you receive dozens of unsolicited emails, and do you feel relieved and reassured to know that your name, buying habits and personal preferences are being tracked, analysed and used by complete strangers?

The answer is probably – no.

The reaction in our house when we receive telesales calls after 6 pm (selling anything from financial services to window blinds) is to ask the caller for their home telephone number so that we can call then back when it is convenient for us. The fact that no one has yet responded to our suggestion that we put this new 'friendship' on a more even footing suggests that something is not quite right. (I used to think that this level of intimacy was irritating, until the other day when I received an unsolicited email offering to increase the size of my penis. I was amazed. I wanted to reply, I had so many questions to ask: Did he really think an unsolicited email was the best way to introduce himself? Had he tested his product on himself? Does size really matter? Fortunately, wiser heads prevailed and I deleted it, but he still keeps emailing me ...)

If someone follows you around town and stands behind you in every shop that you visit, you are entitled to call the police and possibly seek a restraining order. However, if someone analyses the books you buy – or any purchases that you make – on-line, you are supposed to embrace this as a wonderful service. Marketers measure and classify people in ABC groups, segmenting and targeting them, all the time striving to meet their needs. (I was once asked by a database marketing colleague if he could see our customers broken down by age and sex. I replied that most of them were already.) Customer-centricity is the order of the day and everything that businesses do is geared to tracking the needs of customers, creating products and niches, and above all satisfying the customer. Billions of dollars are spent every year on CRM software designed to help corporations with these tasks, and while for some firms their results may be better than before and outdo their competitors', it seems far from certain that their results are as good as they *could* be. Grimly, *seriously*, with narrow *conformity*, they seek to know their customers better.

Often, customers – you and me – are treated like bullies. We have all the power because we have money to spend, the power to spend it, and the ability to influence the expenditure of others. Companies, who play the role of victim, crave all these. They try not to upset the bullies, striving for their friendship and loyalty and wanting some of our power, so that they too can become powerful.

To put it simply, companies are not only nervous of their competitors – they also act as if they are afraid of their customers, both current and potential. This is not the basis for a healthy relationship. It is limited and anxious. Anxiety betraying its basis in a serious motivational state. Its 'seriousness' in turn betraying that the relationship contains an ulterior dimension that makes the consumer uneasy.

When firms are afraid of their customers, which for some of them is all of the time, they try to be nice; they are obsequious, ubiquitous, insincere and unbearable. The approach taken to running organisations is geared to customers being right, powerful and needing to feel loved. An example of this is the European telecoms companies who during 2000 paid their governments billions to purchase 3G licences because that's what they thought their customers would want. Burdened with crippling debts, they then discover that exploiting these licences will be prohibitively expensive and – worst of all – unlikely to recoup the original investment from customers in anything like a sensible timeframe. The result of firms' fear of their customers is that marketing and sales strategies are frequently constrained and limited. The only reason that prevents this fact from doing greater harm to businesses is that are all facing the same situation. The dire nature of this situation is recognised by Professor Stephen Brown, writing in the *Harvard Business Review*:

> A mindless devotion to customers means me-too products, copycat advertising campaigns and marketplace stagnation.[1]

Compounding this is a touching belief in the dependability and predictability of customers. But customers often simply do not know what they want; in fact, they don't even know what they *don't* want. The real truth is that they are essentially inconsistent. This is highlighted by the ultimate success of many products that were initially rejected by focus groups – from Sony's Walkman to the Chrysler minivan.

More than that, customers do not necessarily want to be researched, and they certainly don't want insincerity in the guise of building customer loyalty and relationship marketing. Respect, value, efficiency, genuine understanding and a positive approach, but not insincerity. Many of the most successful product launches and marketing campaigns of recent years have either ignored the standard market practices, or have resulted from a deep, genuine understanding of what people actually want; a much deeper understanding than might emerge from a focus group, for example.

Motivationally rich motorbiking

There is a huge difference between creating a genuine relationship and pandering to imagined customer needs. What are needed are relationships that engage several motivational states in innovative and rewarding ways. An organisation that went out of its way to creating a special relationship with its customers is Harley-Davidson and its Harley Owners' Group (HOG).

Imagine a long-established business brand in a highly competitive market, faced with declining sales and a sustained assault from competitors generally regarded as more innovative, cheaper and better. Many businesses have, of course, faced similar situations, and while there is no quick-fix solution, a successful turnaround is certainly more likely to be achieved with imagination and audacity. Clearly, continuing as before is not a sustainable option: organisations need people who can be creative and innovative enough to find a new route to sales success.

This situation faced Harley-Davidson, a firm that had enjoyed a long history as the USA's foremost motorbike manufacturer. Founded in 1903, Harley-Davidson is today the only major US motorcycle producer. The company experienced hard times in the late 1960s and 1970s, and by the early 1980s its reputation and business were in serious trouble following a sustained onslaught from affordable, high-quality Japanese machines produced by companies such as Honda and Kawasaki. However, the business recovered and flourished after employees bought the firm from its owner in 1981. Despite the global economic downturn, Harley-Davidson achieved its sixteenth consecutive year of record revenues and earnings in 2001, and this performance seems set to continue. A glance at its financial results highlights the strength and improving performance of the business (Table 9.1).

Table 9.1 Harley-Davidson's financial performance

	1997	1998	1999	2000	2001
Revenues, US$ m	1,763	2,064	2,453	2,906	3,363
Net profit, US$ m	174	214	267	348	438
Earnings per share, US$	0.56	0.69	0.86	1.13	1.43
Share price, US$ (fiscal year close)	13.63	23.69	32.03	39.75	54.31
Return on shareholders' equity, per cent	23.4	23.0	24.4	27.1	27.7

Source: Economist Intelligence Unit

Harley-Davidson is now America's leading bike manufacturer, with an amazing 90 per cent of customers staying loyal to the company. True, it might seem easy to sell a product as exciting and appealing as a motor-bike. But then Harley-Davidson also manages to get tens of thousands of its customers to keep on buying its machines, as well as paying to attend rallies where they enjoy themselves, make friends, provide valuable customer feedback – and even tattoo themselves with the name of the company! How many businesses achieve that?

It is valuable to understand how this turnaround happened. Harley-Davidson benefited from ideas that at the time were bold and different in three areas: improving design, improving product quality, and most spec-tacularly of all, genuinely bonding with its customers.

■ *Design innovation* has been a keystone of Harley-Davidson's success, and epitomises how it constantly pushed at expectations, sometimes successfully, sometimes less so. The company consistently produces models that advance the aesthetics and technology of the motorcycle. The V-Rod, a liquid-cooled model introduced in 2001, was an instant hit, winning numerous industry awards.

■ *Product quality* started to improve when senior managers had the opportunity to visit Honda's Marysville, Ohio motorcycle facility. The difference they saw between that facility and their own was dramatic in terms of layout, production flow, efficiency and inventory management. The management concluded that if Harley was going to be competitive with Honda and the other Japanese motorcycle manufacturers, it would have to effect a business-wide, just-in-time manufacturing initiative called MAN – materials as needed. Production operations were moved together, and Harley was able to cut the amount of inventories received too early, and reduce the amount of space required to manufacture its product. As it later turned out, it was creating space for additional production.

■ *Sales and customer loyalty* has provided the most startling area of innovation and success for Harley-Davidson. There are several methods that the company uses to bond with its customers; underpinning each has been an approach that understands each individual customer and sells the spirit of riding a Harley, providing a knowledgeable approach that appeals to customers' emotions. The managers of the business meet their customers regularly at rallies, where new models can be sampled with free demonstration rides. Advertising reinforces the image and perception of owning a Harley, appealing as much to existing customers to stay loyal as to attract new ones. The Harley Owners' Group (HOG) activities are central to binding its customers to the company, and rather than providing trite or cheap benefits Harley devotes considerable resources to ensuring that its customers receive benefits that they value. Membership of HOG is free for the first year for new Harley owners, thereafter a membership fee is payable; over two-thirds of their customers renew.

Rich Teerlink, former Chairman and CEO of Harley-Davidson, highlights two factors contributing to the firm's successful renaissance:

Perhaps the most significant program was – and continues to be – the Harley Owners' Group (HOG), created in 1983. Begun as a way to communicate more effectively with the company's end users, HOG quickly grew into the world's largest motorcycle club. And dealers [a vital customer group and sales channel] regained confidence that Harley could and would be a dependable partner.

What Harley is doing through HOG is to engineer and manage its 'motivational proposition', expressing its 'brand' in the reciprocal terms of a true relationship. It also understood that the key to a true relationship was more than packaging and presentation – but something that would involve all the workforce:

I myself didn't have a plan for the company in my back pocket. I only knew that capturing the ideas of our people – all the people at Harley – was critical to our future success.[2]

Time and again in our own work and that of our colleague Dr Mitzi Desselles (see below) we have seen clear evidence of this link between organisational climate, individual motivation and customer impact. If you want to build great relationships with your customers you must do the same with your employees.

Unlike many firms, Harley-Davidson was afraid of neither its customers nor its employees, a rarity in corporate circles. Furthermore, Harley-Davidson and other businesses expose the fallacy among many marketing professionals that they could not possibly get to know all of their customers. Harley is one company selling tens of thousands of machines, but it does this in a way that lets the CEO (and anyone else in the firm) come face to face regularly with many of its customers. Not a bad idea.

This motivationally rich relationship means that customers have an unprecedented loyalty to the Harley brand. The 8,000 employees of Harley-Davidson successfully promote the idea that they do more than make a product of rubber and metal – they market mystique and fulfil dreams. The appeal of its products and the genius of its marketing strategy are proved by the firm's long-term financial performance, sustaining demand for both the company's products and its shares.

Harley-Davidson is an exception. For much of the time the situation we find is one where obsequious firms are irritating busy, uncertain customers. This uncertainty only serves to make firms more desperate, insincere and obsequious, which in turn leads to greater irritation and uncertainty. And so the cycle persists. A few firms that are genuinely audacious, stoking up demand for products and providing genuine value for customers, break this hopeless and depressing situation.

For many more organisations customers represent a 'dangerous edge' over which lie cost and confusion.

Treating customers as real people: the final frontier

Much of marketing and sales is based upon simple and somewhat strange perceptions of human nature. Some of these oddities are easy to discern – such as the idea that I have to be called and presented with something I want to buy (from financial services to window blinds), rather than deciding myself what it is I want. Other ideas are much more ingrained but equally peculiar. There are several common ones.

The first fallacy is that life must *always* be simple for consumers, and the simpler the better. Product, price, place (position) and promotion are seen as essential, and marketing's role is to make people aware of products, providing them in a timely manner, available when and where they are wanted at a price people are prepared to pay. This may be necessary for some businesses, but what about the opposite approach – don't call us, we'll call you? What is wrong with limiting availability, heightening expectations, delaying gratification and nurturing an air of excited unattainability? This approach appeals to customer emotions too, and is likely to resonate with other motivational states previously left untouched. It recognises that marketing doesn't just serve demand – it creates it. It understands that customers are marketing savvy, supremely capable of seeing through CRM-inspired tactics. It is invariably new, wowing customers by showing them something they have not seen before. For sure, customers may also value a relationship with vendors for certain products and at certain times, but what about those moments when they don't want to feel stalked but would rather be wowed?

There are a few examples of customer demand being actively, boldly created. Film companies do it all the time, giving trailers of their films but often keeping the story lines under wraps, releasing teasers and photo stills of the film set instead. This happened during production of the *Star Wars* prequel, *The Phantom Menace*, as well as *The Lord of the Rings*. When the second Harry Potter novel was published, huge secrecy surrounded every aspect of the book, including its title. Two weeks before official publication some copies in the US were 'mistakenly' sold to children by one retail outlet, resulting in a wave of publicity. In truth, the publishers could not lose. Having created such intense secrecy and excitement, if it went all the way to the self-proclaimed 'Harry Potter Day', then that would be an exciting event, and if news leaked, then that too would excite.

It takes audacity and boldness to create a motivationally rich relationship with your customers which must be paradoxical and uncertain. It takes courage to appeal to people's innate curiosity, respect for ingenuity and the unusual, and their need for excitement.

In 1994 when Tango wanted to launch a new, non-carbonated version of its orange juice in the UK, it ran an ad campaign in a public service format. This warned viewers that some outlets were selling knock-off imitations of its brand detectable because they were not fizzy, and asking for these rogue outlets to be reported by calling a free phone number. Some 30,000 people phoned, only to be told that they had been 'Tango'd' as part of the promotion for the company's new, uncarbonated drink. Although reprimanded by the UK Independent Television Commission for abusing the public service information format, Tango had succeeded in generating awareness and appearing irreverent – and hence cool to its market of young drinkers. Now, whenever you are suckered in the UK, it is invariably accompanied with the cry that 'you've been Tango'd!' Certainly it was an ingenious, cool and distinctive way to sell yet another orange juice.

The second fallacy of sales is closely linked to the first, and it is the belief that people will always want products to be understandable and transparent. Prevailing logic suggests that people understand that secrecy is required in certain situations, for example when it relates to a firm's intellectual property, but otherwise they want to know the benefits first, *and* the product features as well. So what about Coca-Cola and Kentucky Fried Chicken, both of whom have guarded their product contents in a shroud of mystery for as long as possible? These are things that we put into our bodies with amazing frequency, and yet we aren't certain about what they contain! Of course, the reason for this is that both firms are using secrecy to develop an exclusive, differentiating appeal for their product among their customers.

Fortunately, intrigue, excitement and secrecy are more widely recognised methods of generating sales than manipulation. Questions such as 'What could it be?' and 'Why is it so secret?' engage and intrigue customers, harnessing the power of their own imagination. This is all about playfulness and rebellion, not serious (rational) conforming. But to do this requires a boldness and confidence that is often missing.

In a playful state, surprise and outrage are also valuable tools for marketing and selling, they have the great advantage of appealing to emotions and amplifying the product by creating excitement. Mike Apter has noted that in a playful state, emotions that are normally negative (anger, fear and so on) are experienced positively – which is why people enjoy horror films. This is a significant, little explored area of the customer relationship that organisations may do well to exploit. Renault recently launched its new model in the UK with an advertising campaign highlighting the car's rear end, and in a frankly outrageous (and very funny) advertisement featuring a range of wiggling bottoms, it linked its new car to people's posteriors. In doing so, the ad was distinctive and memorable; it made the link between the car and comfort and showed that it was fun as well. In fact, many of the ads we remember best are outrageous, a classic example being Benetton's United Colors Campaign featuring startling and provocative images. It was not necessarily beloved, but it certainly made the brand stand out and intrigued people. I remember that having seen the ad I actually visited a Benetton shop – not something I have done before or since – just because I was intrigued by its campaign and wanted to know exactly what it was that it sold.

Professor Stephen Brown arguing in a similar vein, advocates instead what he calls *retromarketing* – a return to the good old days when marketers did not love you, they conned you instead. Customers know you only want their money, so get real and don't pretend to be their best friend.

In Brown's view, the four Ps of retromarketing are perturb, puzzle, perplex and perhaps. The five forces are flim, flam, flirt, fiddle and finagle. This may seem a little extreme, but it does have several clear advantages over the present mantra that the 'customer is always right' and 'we need to build customer loyalty':

- Customers may not want to be loyal, they may not even want to be bothered. So get their interest in new, exciting and engaging ways.
- Customers do not always (or even often) know what they want. So tell them loudly and create demand, don't just serve it.
- Customers want to enjoy themselves and will respond well to the values that they hold dear. So appeal to previously untapped emotions, such as intrigue and excitement, and genuinely *wow* them.

The irony is that marketing managers believe their own hype: they actually think that if you love the customer enough, and tell them you love them, and give them little tokens of your love – then the customer will love you back. Sadly, if all you had to do to love someone was *tell* them, then the world would be a very different place. It may be important at times but much more is required: audacity that inspires the emotions. If Harley-Davidson can consistently persuade its customers to tattoo themselves with the name of its firm, and Tango can introduce a new word to the *Oxford English Dictionary*, then isn't it time your customers got Tango'd?

But love is ... the safest thing

If your partner was serious, conforming, sympathetic and focused on their significant other (you), wouldn't you be, well, bored?

Customers respond to many, many things, yet firms seem to emphasise one single approach – to keep telling you they love you. Why do they persist with this single approach? Perhaps 'love' is the safest thing, perhaps they think it is the best way for them to succeed, because it is safe (no one ever gets angry with someone who keeps saying they love you) – and because everyone else is doing it. Sales techniques need sometimes to be radically different, and for those that can get past the fear factor and do it well, they are likely to find significant success.

The benefits of a slightly different approach are highlighted by the case of Ansett NZ Airlines, which faced the challenge of getting members of its Golden Wing frequent flyer club to renew their annual membership at a price of $300. Its renewal notices enclosed one white Golden Wing sock, with an entertaining letter promising two more on receipt of payment. The reason it offered two more was so that when one goes missing in the laundry (a fate that ultimately befalls all pairs of socks) people still had two to wear. The promotion appealed to a human desire for completion, but most of all Ansett impressed people with its wit. This had two important effects: first, membership renewals soared to 92 per cent, and second, the airline started looking like a business with a personality, interesting and engaging current customers and increasing its appeal to new customers.[3]

The challenge for firms is to get to motivationally understand their customers. Many companies have become skilled at the art of customer relationship management, collecting reams and gigabytes of data about preferences and behaviour, dividing customers into ever finer segments until they are effectively stalking as many of us individually as possible, refining their products and sales pitches to match. But still, these techniques can fall some way short of adequately understanding customers. This is because they are focused only on the points where the customer encounters the company. What matters, and what is often either ignored or totally misunderstood, is the broad context in which the customer is selecting, buying and using their product. If firms genuinely want to impress customers, deepen loyalty and increase sales, then understanding the customer's motivation is vital.

Consider a simple example. Two customers go into a shop looking to buy new washing machines. To the sales manager who serves them they both seem identical, but their situations are entirely different. The first shopper needs a new washing machine to replace an old machine that fell apart that morning. Her priority is to get a new machine in her house and washing the load of clothes for herself and her young family as soon as possible; she does not have time to browse. The second shopper is moving into a new apartment next week, she has time to browse, comparing features and prices, and is in fact interested in finding out about other household appliances as well. If treated the same way, the sales manager may miss out on significant sales opportunities. The first shopper values speed, and will pay a premium price for delivery to solve her current crisis, whereas the second shopper is much less inclined to go for a quick sale, but she may be a candidate for 'relationship building'. This might include a free consulting service, a comprehensive plan for all the appliances needed for the new apartment, a tailored delivery schedule and a modest discount for the volume purchased.

The problem is that without genuinely getting to know each customer's situation, the sales manager can only provide a one-size-fits-all service. It may seem obvious to say that understanding a customer's motivation is central to enhancing sales, but this is frequently frustrated by two factors: firms' fear of really getting to understand their customers, and consequently their limited understanding of the range of motivational states affecting behaviour. Reversal theory actually provides a useful framework for understanding customers' motivations. To understand your customers better try understanding their motivational state at specific times, but remember that these states can reverse or switch:

■ Are the customers motivated by the means or the end? Do they want to achieve a specific goal (suggesting the serious state), as in the case of the shopper urgently needing a new washing machine? Or are they more interested in the journey, wanting enjoyment and experiencing actions (such as browsing) as valuable in their own right? If they favour the latter approach, then this suggests a playful motivational state and can be supported so that when they decide to buy they come to their favourite shop.

■ Do they have a basic sense of wanting to belong (such as the members of Harley-Davidson's Owners' Group), in which case they may be conforming; or are they more interested in feeling different and distinctive – in which case their motivation is to challenge and rebel? Or both at different times?

■ How do they feel about transactions – do they prefer to be in control and dominate (suggesting the mastery state), or do they tend to emphasise personal relationships and openness (showing the sympathy state)?

■ Usually, relationships will be experienced in terms of what is happening to the customers themselves (the self-oriented motivational state). However, there are many products that are bought where the basic motivation is a desire to care for and support other people or objects. Whether I am buying a family holiday, health insurance for my family or cat food, as a customer I am evaluating what is happening primarily in terms of its effects on those I interact with rather than myself – suggesting the other-oriented motivational state.

Of course, reversal theory takes us a step further. Customers, whether they are consumers or other businesses, are not static. Innovative psychologist and market researcher Dr Mitzi Desselles comments that:

> Consumers are not statues. They are more like dancers moving in patterns through different states.[4]

Audacious organisations, those with the awareness and confidence to really connect with their customers, will work to understand how people move through different motivational states. They will start to understand what triggers a reversal, why different pairs of states are important at different times, how to build the protective frames enabling 'bad' emotions to be experienced positively.

Instinctively, we understand these issues at an individual level.

It reminds me of the time I went to my first party as an adolescent. I was there with the other lads, looking at the girls, talking about them, worrying about things like our appearance and personal hygiene, and generally trying to impress. Sadly, the last thing any of us felt able to do was actually get to *know* them. Of course, the few who had the courage and made the effort to do this were the heroes, and – if their later lurid tales were to be believed – they received the benefits of first-mover advantage.

Notes

1   Brown, S. (2001) Torment Your Customers (They'll Love It), *Harvard Business Review*, October
2   Teerlink, R. and Ozley, L. (2000) *More Than a Motorcycle: The Leadership Journey at Harley-Davidson*, Cambridge, MA, Harvard Business School Press
3   For more information on this campaign, and for other inventive and interesting marketing ideas, see Rapp, S. and Collins, T.L. (1998) *Send 'Em One White Sock*, McGraw-Hill, New York
4   Comment made to the authors

CHAPTER TEN

Building a New Eden – Audacity at Work

Work like you don't need the money
Love like you've never been hurt
Dance like nobody's watching
Sing like nobody's listening
Live like it's heaven on earth.

A verse at the entrance to The Eden Project in Cornwall, UK, highlighting the nature of freedom and the essence of audacity

In March 2001, the world's largest conservatories opened; The Eden Project was the culmination of an audacious vision that Tim Smit and his team refused to let die. It is a story of the effort and determination required to turn dreams into reality. But, more than that, it is about having the courage and vision to formulate a dream – to be audacious – in the first place. In the case of The Eden Project, this required life-changing decisions, an ability to see beyond the horizon and an unfailing belief in oneself. As Tim Smit himself says:

No one has a monopoly on dreams, but only a rare few discover the alchemist's art of making them real. Making things real demands… a single-mindedness and determination to succeed that persuades others as much by the force of your conviction as by the idea itself.[1]

Realising dreams means being wilful, not taking 'no' for an answer, and tenaciously jumping the many hurdles that block the road ahead. It requires the audacity factor, awareness, deep motivational connection and confidence.

About The Eden Project

- The Eden Project opened in St Austell, Cornwall, in March 2001, with a mission 'To promote the understanding and responsible management of the vital relationship between plants, people and resources leading to a sustainable future for all'.[2] The purpose of The Eden Project is to make plant-based issues interesting to ordinary people. It is specifically designed to engage the public at large, educating, amusing, delighting and informing.

- It contains over 100,000 plants, representing 5,000 species from many of the climatic zones of the world. Although many of these can grow in the mild conditions of Cornwall in the west of England, others demand greenhouses and are grown in Eden's two gigantic conservatories.

- The Humid Tropics Biome houses rainforest plants such as bananas, rubber, cocoa, coffee, teak and mahogany. It stands 15,590 metres square (1.55 hectares), 55 metres high, 100 metres wide and 200 metres long.

- The Warm Temperate Biome is filled with the plants of the Mediterranean regions of the world, including South Africa, California and the Mediterranean itself. Outside sunflowers, hemp, tea and a host of other plants from the temperate region grow. It stands 6,540 metres square (0.65 hectares), 35 metres high, 65 metres wide and 135 metres long.

- The biomes are made of hexagons, each approximately nine metres across. The frame is constructed from galvanised tubular steel, glazed with a transparent, recyclable foil that should last at least 30 years. It is self-cleaning, anti-static, very strong, transparent to UV light and is not degraded by sunlight. The whole structure is guaranteed maintenance-free for at least 25 years.

- The Eden Project has already started a small breeding programme to maintain stocks of endangered conifers, and expects to showcase what other Botanical Institutes are doing to breed endangered species.

- In addition to the plants, art is central to Eden's ethos and way of presenting nature, and from the outset there have been artistic expressions of storytelling across the site. Furthermore, Eden is a place that is constantly growing and changing, and the use of the word Project in the name reflects the dynamic nature of Eden.

- The venture is owned by The Eden Charitable Trust who have set up Eden Project Limited to build, run and administer it, and ensure the commercial profits that will guarantee its future. It is located 30 miles west of Plymouth and 15 west of Bodmin – about 270 miles west of London. Fifty miles further west is Land's End.

- By mid-March 2002, The Eden Project's first birthday, it had attracted 1.91 million visitors against an original plan of 750,000.
- The Eden Project has had a significant effect on the wider community, generating substantial economic and other benefits. It currently employs 600 people, 50 per cent of whom were previously unemployed, in one of the UK's most depressed regions. To date, The Eden Project has attracted almost four million visitors, benefiting a large number of businesses in the region and creating around 1,700 full-time jobs in the wider area (Cornwall, Devon and parts of Somerset).
- The Eden Project is a major educational resource, working in partnership with local schools, colleges and universities.
- The original idea for The Eden Project came from Tim Smit, who believes:

> The way we treat plants and work with them is the story of the planet. Decisions we make now will materially affect the way our children and our children's children live and thrive (or not) on this fragile planet.
>
> The Eden Project is a showcase for all the questions and many of the answers. But Eden is not a worthy, over-serious guilt ridden place; nor does it preach. It is about education and communication of the major environmental issues of the day always presented in an engaging, involving, even humorous way.[1]

The dream of Eden

In the late 1980s, Tim Smit and his family decided to change their lives. Dissatisfied with the excessive travelling that dominates musicians' lives, he left London for Cornwall. Originally intending to create a recording studio and work from home, Smit's plans were to change after a chance encounter. Early in 1990, his builder renovating their Cornish home, John Nelson, invited Tim Smit to look around an old estate. The secretive, overgrown and unkempt walled gardens he found captured his imagination, and this first project was to lead, eventually, to the development of The Eden Project.

> There, under a shroud of bramble, survived a solitary old vine, snaking in and out of the broken panes of glass... defiant against the onslaught of decay. Hanging on a nail in the wall were the vine scissors... in the valley below the Big House, we were to find the remains of a sub-tropical garden, choked into dank submission by self-seeded ash, sycamore and willow. Something inside me told me that this was what I had been waiting for.[1]

Tim Smit and his colleagues set about restoring these Lost Gardens of Heligan to their former glory. The desire to pick up those vine scissors was all-consuming, as was the enormity of the task that lay ahead. Like the surviving vine, dreams need to withstand the onslaught of obstructive reality.

The Lost Gardens of Heligan took six years to complete with the help of expert volunteers. The aim was to create a working garden as it used to be – not simply a showpiece. Sometimes, this attitude and vision resulted in a direct collision with other interested parties, each with their own agenda or traditional conventions.

Clearly, the more formidable the odds and the greater the challenges, the more daunting and difficult it is to continue pursuing a dream. Strength and conviction are undoubtedly needed to overcome the obstacles; society is not often welcoming to challenge or change, but with a wilful tenacity can come to learn their value in time. This is not a misplaced faith or obsession, but rather an individual's conviction borne of their own personality and driven by their own motivation. Signs of the eight motivational states forming the foundation of audacity were already on display: serious at times, playful at others; conforming and rebellious, masterful and sympathetic, focused on succeeding oneself but also clearly focused on understanding and working with others.

As the saying goes, 'nothing succeeds like success'. Restoring the gardens rejuvenated the local economy, with restaurants, shops and local businesses all benefiting from the popularity of the gardens. While working on the gardens at Heligan, Tim Smit, Philip McMillan Browse and John Nelson were looking for sites to place a conservatory for exotic plants. Finding a large quarry sparked an idea about something grander: constructing the largest conservatories ever built for plants from around the world. This would prove a significant aesthetic and educational resource, a commercial venture, and an inspiration.

The Eden Project is an example of a dream whose enormity almost defied the imagination. When dreams are smaller in size and more manageable, the hurdles can seem, with effort, surmountable. When the dream is so large that the top of the hurdles can't even be seen, there must be a potent blend of motivational richness if the vision is not to evaporate. The Eden Project is just such an example. Although most of us would never undertake such a large project against all the odds, the experiences of those involved show that many of the obstacles faced by others in trying to turn their dreams into reality require seeing the challenge through different motivational lenses: focusing on milestones (serious), maintaining energy (playful), ensuring capability (mastery), fostering great relationships (sympathy) and so on. It was the way that Tim Smit utilised these motivational perspectives and the behaviours they promote that made the journey to Eden so successful.

Creating Eden

The Eden Project would require a great deal of money that Tim Smit and his team did not have – some estimates topped £100 million (the actual cost was nearer £86 million). It might not even be possible to build it, and the potential difficulties seemed overwhelming. Indeed, thinking about the many daunting tasks that lay ahead would probably have deterred many from pursuing their ideas. However, Smit's audacious approach had several important factors that ensured success.

A band of fellow travellers

Large projects rely on the strengths, skills and collaboration of many talented people. The mixture of skills results in progress, and expertise in all areas, practical, technical, creative and financial, is necessary. Gathering the right people around you can be difficult and is fraught with uncertainty. An idea that seems exciting to you may simply appear impossible – even absurd – to others. What is striking about the team Smit built around him was its diversity of backgrounds, personalities and perspectives; a team with more than a few members of the 'awkward squad' capable of bringing real grit, focus and creativity to the Project. As The Eden Project shows, support was gained as much through the sheer, relentless brute force of determination, energy, excitement and belief, as through any specific arguments. In short, a performance climate was born.

At first sight, it appears to be a stroke of great good fortune that The Eden Project attracted so many enthusiastic, talented and strong people, with almost boundless energy. In fact, the team built gradually, one by one, with the belief and commitment of the early 'co-conspirators' escalating the Project and providing a secure bedrock upon which to build a team and develop support. Tim Smit promotes the Tinkerbell Theory, where, like the fairy in *Peter Pan*, something really can exist if enough people believe strongly enough in it. This infectious phenomenon was to prove crucial to the success of their plans.

Building a confidence frame

Tim Smit built a climate in which everyone involved in The Eden Project believed passionately in the value of the plan. Encouraged by the success of rebuilding the Lost Gardens of Heligan, they had hope and belief. However, Smit acknowledges that they did not fully appreciate what actually lay ahead. It was a step into the unknown. He feels this was beneficial, with the lessons learned gradually and obstacles tackled individually or in manageable groups as the Project progressed, rather than hitting them all at once and causing the team to abandon the venture.

Soon, however, all plans need to focus on detailed, practical aspects of implementation, and The Eden Project was no exception. The immense demands of such a large Project quickly turned thoughts from the idyllic dream and excited plans to harsher realities.

Crucially, however, the feelings of freedom and excitement that came with the original vision of Eden were not constrained. It was precisely the motivations and behaviour that led Smit and his team to embark on the Project in the first place – feelings of mastery, mutual support and rebelliousness – that came into their own when it was necessary to deal with the myriad complexities of practical details. Although undoubtedly a leader, Smit encouraged leadership in others and sometimes followed advice he was not completely happy with. This is tough – it demands respect for and trust in others. He had the self-awareness that it would be unwise not to recognise when he was out of his depth and when the assistance of specialists was required. Here, calling on contacts is highly useful; introductions via networks can be invaluable. Construction matters, acquiring a location, financial difficulties, legal aspects, developing a business plan to attract funding and many operational considerations made the plans reel from one difficulty to the next. Only a real self-confidence and heightened serious state kept Tim Smit on track, as the end goal was always foremost in his thinking.

Feasibility studies were needed to gain financial and technical support. Clearly, the world of business, with its own agenda and interests, would need to be considered. This was a particularly difficult path for the team. A naturally rebellious orientation does not take easily to the demands of conformity. Yet, conformist skills would be required if the plan was to progress. The aims of The Eden Project were to come into direct confrontation with opposing, external views. Members of the Trust set up to oversee the Project, and other members of the team, feared the incursion of minority business interests into the plans. With such large projects requiring huge sums of money, questions of funding, ownership and control were an inevitable hurdle. A degree of compromise was necessary to secure funding from, among others, The European Development Fund and The Millennium Commission, and to obtain a bank guarantee. Also, instead of the five biospheres originally conceived, financial pressures meant that only two were possible – otherwise, the Project would have collapsed. The team, in arriving at a compromise, not only kept the Project alive but also retained the option to add the other biospheres in the future. In doing this, they realised they could not totally control the situation but instead changed the way they contributed within it.

In seeking funds from Europe, they came up against opposition from other bids, claiming that less money would be available for other parts of the south west of England if a large sum was given to The Eden Project. This was a serious challenge. The area had been awarded £150 million from the EU for regeneration; a limited sum pitched project against project and county against county. The leader of Somerset County Council, Humphrey Temperley, believed so strongly in the importance of The Eden Project for the whole region that he gave a passionate and galvanising speech, asking everyone to support it regardless of which county they lived in. He withdrew one of his own bids for a project in Somerset, which caused others to withdraw their opposition to The Eden Project.

Building the climate for success

A great deal of effort was required to secure local support. Tim Smit and his team knew that no matter how much financial and technical support could be gained elsewhere, the whole Project would be seriously threatened – and probably collapse – without support from the local community. This was to prove a particular challenge with many highs and lows. The team worked tirelessly to persuade the local community of their ideas and the importance of the Project for the local area and for Cornwall as a whole. This meant listening actively to all concerns and addressing them patiently, imaginatively and courteously. The Eden team understood that circumventing or skimping on this process would be ultimately futile, as agencies that lend or donate money to projects would be much, much more reluctant to do so if the spectre of local opposition was looming. This may seem self-serving, but is more likely to spring from the ethos of the Project: working together honestly and openly, showing trust and respect.

The journey – dealing with frustration

The struggle to raise money caused immense and constant frustration. When his dream had to confront tough questions from people who did not share or understand the nature of what they were trying to achieve, Tim Smit often felt enraged and frustrated. Having to function in a world that plays by standardised, one-size-fits-all rules, where conservatism and prudence mix with scepticism and cynicism, is wearing, and made him feel constrained. While Smit's rebellious nature was ever present, always keeping the dream alive and helping to suggest imaginative arguments and solutions, he also recognised the need to work within the system. In this way he showed his serious motivational state, focusing on the need for progress and achievement, and also an ability to conform, using the financial support as a sign of approval, a gathering snowball that would help overcome future opposition.

Tim Smit drew on aspects of his own character that helped deal successfully with frustration, arguing the merits of working with business rather than against it. Although a culture clash and ideological differences can emerge, the point is that both sides can understand each other and work together. A direct confrontation would not have helped, and he needed to deal positively with the frustration. Smit was often surprised at how many executives would express their personal support for the aims of the Project, saying that they, too, would like to see their companies pursuing projects that could also make a difference to the world, but that they felt constrained and unable to do so. A theme repeated throughout his experiences, Tim Smit bemoans the almost complete stranglehold that shareholders and governments exert, preventing new approaches with goals that are other than financial.

Tim Smit found that his honesty in preparing figures for fund-raising resulted in his deep frustration. He was unaware, for example, that others would automatically and quite arbitrarily reduce his estimates by 20 per cent, significantly affecting his ability to raise the necessary level of funding. He believes that this simply 'institutionalises deception'. The schism between the real world and the world of ideals is often difficult to reconcile. Why such actions, perceived as deception, should be necessary, would try the logic of an idealist. Moreover, this can cause a plan to dwindle in scope to the point where it becomes so ordinary that the dream is all but lost. This risk-aversion is contrary to the wilful, pioneer spirit, without which civilisation would be unable to progress. Tim Smit increasingly saw the parts of the worlds of science and art as having compromised their ideals for business and political agendas.

The funding gap was huge, indicating that at least one million visitors would be required just to meet the interest payments on the loan. During the development, crunch time was fast approaching, with funds drying up rapidly, despite companies and individuals agreeing to work for nothing or for small sums by way of goodwill, commitment and investment in the Project. In seeking funds, the team approached English Partnership, an organisation responsible for funding regeneration projects. Again, the team found that standard, conventional thinking frustrated their efforts. The team intended using the site of a disused quarry, which they considered a brown-field site. However, it was in the middle of rural Cornwall, and current thinking considered brown sites to be in cities. It took considerable effort to change this view.

One of the essential lessons learnt from The Eden Project is the need to stay strong. Without strength and energy, the ability to keep going may vanish. Even after much hard work preparing and planning, quite possibly over a period of years, sometimes the hardest work remains to be done. As Tim Smit puts it,

> there comes a moment in all great ventures when the talking has to stop... but turning a dream into reality needs iron soul, money in the bank and military organisation.[1]

When spirits flagged, it helped the team members to remind themselves of why they started the Project in the first place.

A tenacious, fighting spirit is essential, as Tim Smit found when repeatedly facing people who didn't understand what Eden was about.

> Why, for God's sake, put yourself and your friends and family through years of grief to build a crappy theme park so that some smart-ass can define it in a sentence? Too many people were putting too much of themselves into this. We weren't for sale. Eden wasn't a product, it was a place in the heart.[1]

The motivation to build Eden

As the experiences of Tim Smit and his colleagues show, while one motivational state can dominate, it is possible – necessary – to flip this state to its opposite pair or another dominant state, so that actions and attitudes remain positive and effective. For example, the rebellious state served Tim Smit very well for challenging existing issues and giving him the belief in self to pursue his goals. However, when needed, he was able to switch to its opposite motivational states of conforming to ensure his plans did not go awry. He acknowledges the need for this when, on a number of occasions, seemingly intractable problems threatened to end The Eden Project, necessitating careful compromise. Although many were concerned that compromise would be the start of the slippery slope, where their hopes and ideas would be overtaken by the interests of the business community, it in fact kept the Project alive to fight another day.

The result may not have been the original one envisioned – this is inevitable for large, protracted projects – but the Project was an unmitigated success. As Tim Smit says,

> Eden never was about plants and architecture, it was always about harnessing people to a dream and exploring what they are capable of.[1]

No one could argue that their achievement was anything less than extraordinary, the odds were against them and they never gave up.

The Eden Project stands as a monument, a tribute to the power of awareness, confidence and motivational connection. The audacity factor is writ large in this project, changing the lives of those who built it and quite possibly many of those who visit it.

The power of challenge and rebellion – and the need to conform

Motivationally it is interesting to see how Eden 'worked'. Clearly, the ability to build the world's largest conservatories suggests the involvement of a team that likes a challenge, and this was already shown by Smit's decision to move from London, and the work done to restore the Lost Gardens of Heligan. However, a common trait evident in many of the individuals who worked on The Eden Project was an ability to constantly question assumptions. When most of those around you are saying 'it can't be done' or 'it has to be this way', it takes a particularly strong and challenging individual to question it. This is not to advocate ignoring others; conversely, it is to advocate listening to everyone, judging who you should heed and being able to admit when you may be wrong or when compromise is needed.

Even so, the divergent aims of the different groups inevitably led to tensions and unease as the plans progressed. Clearly, the greatest challenge is sometimes to accept the opinions of others. This can only occur from a basis of respect and consideration for others – trust is the hallmark of a successful team. As Tim Smit argues, when a project relies heavily on a team and the support of wider groups, such as the local community, it will fail if the views of others are dismissed. This highlights the significance of the conforming state, where the rules and conventions such as those operating within the team are seen as being supportive, and the basic motive is a desire to fit in and accept.

How plans change: the serious and playful states

The original plan was to construct five, linked biospheres – four of them designed to contain plants from different regions of the world. This plan was to change over time as new ideas were added and financial pressures took their toll. A degree of flexibility coupled with a dogged determination not to capitulate is a difficult combination – especially when a dream is personally important – but one that can mean the difference between sudden failure and keeping your dream alive for future success. This need for flexibility highlights the important feature of the serious state. In such a project playfulness is essential. It was the fuel that kept the show on the road. A 'private strategy' which said that there is only one goal and one way would have been doomed to fail. In the serious state we need the maturity to maintain the vision, the desire for achievement, while letting the goals and practicalities evolve and change.

Masterful and sympathetic

During the development of The Eden Project a buoyant sense of mastery was vital. Interactions with others were often experienced as a struggle for control, mastery and domination. The original idea had to win through, not only to avoid getting bogged down but also to prevent the whole Project losing track, and perhaps turning into a giant theme park – not at all its original aim. The basic motive in the mastery state is power rather than being liked, and access to this state was clearly a necessity.

However, the reverse of mastery – the sympathy state – was also clearly an important part of Tim Smit's thinking, with a desire to treat people as people, rather than manipulatively, and get them to give their best to the Project. Coupled with the other-oriented state, where care, concern for others and the Project as a whole, frequently guided actions, the sympathy state was central to Smit's success at building an effective and motivated team. The basic motivation in the sympathy state is a desire to develop relationships based on openness and affection. Interestingly, this sympathetic approach was mirrored in the ethos of the Project's goals: where harmony and co-operation could lead to a new way of living.

There is an interesting symmetry in the fact that The Eden Project itself is both a masterful achievement, a clear example of the power of vision and ingenuity, while at the same time being a development sympathetic to the needs of its customers, the environment and its original objectives. Just as The Eden Project itself is masterful and sympathetic, so were the people who built it.

The importance of others – and oneself

When needed, Tim Smit and his team clearly had the ability to evaluate developments primarily in terms of their effects on the Project, the teams and their goals, rather than interpreting events solely for their impact on themselves. This is the importance of other-orientation. The Eden Project always aspired to be greater than the sum of its parts, which is necessarily at odds with self-promotion. Concern for others, honesty and trust enabled everyone to feel valued and work effectively together. Further than this The Eden Project has a 'transcendent' quality which leads everyone to feel part of something bigger than themselves – a spiritual, elusive 'other' which we can also grasp at. But even with this, such a project also allows each one involved to intensively focus on themselves, to make a unique contribution, to learn something special.

The importance of Eden

Tim Smit clearly values audacity. During his schooldays, he disliked discipline and orders, valuing instead respect and consideration for individuals and ideas. Reading about the development of The Eden Project, it is clear that breaking free from the constraints of society is necessary to realise dreams and potential. This is so, because society limits thinking and actions; it douses the spark of motivation with the cold water of precedence and scepticism. Social norms ignore the fact that audacious dreams, by their nature, often originate from dissatisfaction with the status quo or existing approaches. Tim Smit argues that:

> At one level what Eden could be about is radicalising the Establishment, working with it to arrive at solutions that it couldn't have arrived at on its own because of lack of time, organisational atrophy, vested interests or the absence of lateral thinking. But this is not possible in a vacuum; in order to effect change, all the parties involved in an issue need to have their seat at the table. This is precisely why Eden, if it is to play this role, should be as apolitical as possible.[1]

The rebellious young schoolchild would be proud.

It is easy to criticise Tim Smit's philosophy as being contradictory. His vision rests on the conflicting beliefs of the importance of the individual while at the same time stressing the importance of community. To a lesser extent, there is a further contradiction in The Eden Project itself, which drew on business for funding and relies on its commercial appeal for its continued success, but is designed to further education, understanding and enjoyment of nature. While there are doubtless many personal views and attitudes at play in creating the success of The Eden Project, any contradictions that exist are natural. In different circumstances and at different times, both individuals and communities matter. This mirrors the essential contradictions of reversal theory.

The Eden Project highlights a recipe for audacity, that builds confidence and awareness. This includes:

- Clarity of vision and purpose, being clear in one's own mind what needs to be achieved, and then being guided by a motivationally rich vision. This also helps to make others audacious as well.
- Avoiding exit strategies to safety zones as these undermine commitment and only serve to deflect activities away from the goal. In the development of The Eden Project, commitment was essential to turn ideas into reality. Tim Smit came to understand that

> There comes a quiet moment when you have no audience except the harshest critic of them all: yourself.[1]

- The ability to be wilfully bold – and then to follow through on commitments. Tim Smit emphasises the importance of pushing yourself to achieve by boldly stating your plans to others and to yourself, referring to claims less as lies but as 'telling future truths'.

> The baggage of preconceived ideas about how things should be done has all but atrophied many of the older institutions, burdening them with a specialist, departmental culture. We will fight tooth and nail to ensure that, while Eden has all the expertise that we require, there will never be any academic empire-building here.[1]

- A strong, committed team that is diverse, awkward and confident. In the words of Tim Smit:

> I cannot tell you how proud I feel of the team who rolled their sleeves up and wouldn't admit defeat because they believed that what we were doing was important.

We intended to create something that not only encourages us to understand and to celebrate the world we live in, but also inspires us to action. Eden isn't so much a destination as a place in the heart. It is not just a marvellous piece of science-related architecture; it is also a statement of our passionate belief in an optimistic future for mankind.

... we want you to leave here feeling that we all could make a very real difference to the world we live in if we could work together. In a world of -isms and -ologies, of expertise so refined that only experts understand it, we have brought together scientists, artists and technologists to create a distinctive culture, one that makes the possibilities of the future come to life in a way that we can all comprehend.[1]

Proud of all that his team had accomplished, Tim Smit offers the ultimate praise: ' ... They had done what everyone had said was impossible ...'

■ Not being afraid of the unknown, but rather having the flexibility and courage to explore options. Moreover, an understanding that determination and commitment are not the same as rigidity.

At the opening ceremony of The Eden Project, it was clear that all the hard work bringing the Project to completion was not an ending but a new beginning. This highlights another point about audacity – that once the mould is broken, nothing is unobtainable; fears and doubts give way to self-belief and determination. As Tim Smit argues, if people believe in something it will happen. Challenging convention shows that it only ever served to restrict us and limit our potential. In this way, following the road to audacity is very much a journey of belief. The travel itinerary and destination are of your own choosing, not ones determined by others or convention. This is not to say that the road will always be smooth, but it will always be revealing and rewarding. Being able to be yourself is one of the hardest things to achieve; resisting the forces that act to constrain our dreams and hopes is fundamental to personal success.

The development of The Eden Project highlights a common pitfall for many who sense a niggling dissatisfaction with the status quo and a vague feeling that something else, something important, is waiting to be heard: it is often easier to say no than to say yes. If that is the case, then The Eden Project, and the words at its entrance, may provide inspiration and motivation.

Notes

1   All quotes from Tim Smit are taken from Smit, T. (2001) *Eden*, Corgi Books, London
2   Company profile: No Trouble in Paradise, *Director*, March 2003

CHAPTER ELEVEN

The Road from Morocco

The impulse for this book came in a small room in a tower on the roof of a Kasbah, looking out over the dry, dusty, snow-capped mountains of the High Atlas. I was staying there as the result of a determination to do something totally different to create a more liberating approach to the way organisations regenerate themselves. I was seeking new ideas and places that would stimulate radical and innovative thinking: a place where people could think through what they wanted to achieve and let go of tired assumptions and prejudices.

My colleagues and I had journeyed there shortly after the 9/11 outrage. Some people had been very cautious about our going – this was, after all, an Islamic country, and in their minds was no distance (rather than several thousand miles!) from the Middle East.

The financial markets were panicking and the frothy, silly party days of the dotcom boom were being replaced by a terrible hangover.

All of a sudden, instead of boundaries being broken down, caution, fear and uncertainty were busy building them up. That caution and fear have continued during the whole of the writing of this book. After the excesses of the last ten years, people and organisations have become distrustful and even more cynical.

But where does this caution and cynicism take us? That was the nagging question. Wasn't it precisely in the uncertain, troubled times that we need greater audacity, not less, and a leadership to promote it? What was it that makes some people and some organisations able to respond audaciously, and others not?

And then I began to find out about the Kasbah.

Imlil

Imlil is a cluster of small, poor Berber villages at the foot of Mount Touk-bahl, the highest peak in the region, about 60 km from Marrakech. Electricity didn't arrive here until 1997. Access to the village is via a long, boulder-strewn road, really nothing more than the smoothing of the natural terrain.

The village is set among rugged, brown mountains in a valley where a broad, virtually dry river bed cuts a path almost the width of the valley floor. The area is prone to flash flooding and the floor is covered with the debris of these occasions. In winter, the peaks are covered with snow, while for the rest of the year they are dry, dusty and bare, punctuated by small outcrops of walnut and fruit trees, juniper bushes and tiny parcels of arable land growing barley in pocket handkerchief-sized plots.

Until a few years ago people survived here through subsistence farming and selling walnuts in the market at Marrakech for cash. More recently other cash crops such as apples and cherries have been intro-duced but increasingly the main source of employment has been tourism, providing muleteers and guides to a steady stream of trekkers heading off into the mountains.

The people here are Berbers, a proud and ancient people who speak their own language as well as Arabic and French. Most of the Berbers wear traditional clothes – not for the tourist photographs, which they avoid unless they recognise that a level of trust and mutual respect exists, but because they are simply more comfortable to be dressed like that. The women wear clothes of a modest design but in the most vibrant colours, particularly red and yellow, while the men are more soberly dressed in long cotton or wool djellabahs.

The villages consist of mud or cement-rendered houses, usually haphaz-ardly following narrow twisting paths up the hillside. The air is full of the smells of mules, mint and wood fires. The mint is for mint tea, which is hot, sweet and offered everywhere to friend and stranger alike.

There is an innate respect and warmth for each other, people take time to stop, greet with a handshake and talk to each other. Bartering is common in all transactions but it is based upon mutually discovering the fairest rather than the lowest price.

The Kasbah Du Toukbahl

The Kasbah lies at the top of a 10–15 minute walk above the village. This book was first conceived as I stayed there in one of the little towers on the roof of a restored building that was once one of the houses of the local ruler. It is a place that inspires people not just for where it is, but also for its story and what it stands for.

The Kasbah looks ancient but in fact was only built in the 1940s. It is, however, the product of an earlier, almost medieval, world.

It is built on the site of small hamlet at the edge of Imlil. The local chief – the Caid – bought the people out, and ordered that the village be razed to the ground and the Kasbah built in its place. No one dared argue – the Caid had a dungeon built, could use it on a whim and was not afraid to do so. The Kasbah was a place of which you would be afraid. Villagers were ordered to close the shutters on their houses and not gaze upon the hill when the Caid was in residence; fear and history guaranteed that few disobeyed him.

In 1956, Morocco became independent from France and the Glaoui family, who had ruled the country on behalf of the colonial power, fell. The local Caid disappeared and the Kasbah began to fall into ruins.

Then in 1989 two brothers, Chris and Mike McHugo, travelling through Morocco with their mother after the death of their father, stayed in the village at the foot of the Kasbah. Looking up at the ruin of the old Kasbah, they decided to see if they could buy it. Imlil then was even poorer and less developed than it is now, and this was certainly no rich person's conceit to buy an exotic holiday home – the McHugos had a much more audacious vision.

Mike and Chris are an interesting pair. Chris is very much the well-heeled consultant, formerly with one of the world's largest consultancies and Mike an educator, former bus driver and entrepreneur. They both share, however, a deep love of North Africa and have trekked extensively through the remote and beautiful mountainous terrain that is much of Morocco. In doing so they have built friendships and an understanding of the local people, including that of Omar 'Maurice' Ait Bahmed, a respected leader in the local community and mountain guide whose house they were staying in when the idea of buying the Kasbah first occurred. Omar went on to be one of the key players in creating and enabling the Kasbah to be what it is today.

From the start, the vision was to develop something upon sustainable principles that would benefit both visitors and local inhabitants. It was to be both a successful business and an experiment in social entrepreneurship.

The vision for this place I find astonishing in its motivational richness. It is quoted verbatim:

■ To be a showcase, flagship development for sustainable tourism in a fragile mountain environment.

- To be a viable business involved in the development of the Moroccan economy and its growth.
- To contribute to the enhancement, viability and vitality of the life of the local community (biosphere concept linked with Gross National Happiness).
- To be a centre of excellence for academic work on the High Atlas Berbers and in Morocco.
- To be capable of being an exclusive mountain retreat providing exceptional privacy to almost anyone.
- To continue to generate a change in attitude/thinking in our guests through exposure to something different.
- To be able to modify our corporate behaviour by receiving feedback from the local community.
- To reward stakeholders and create a product they can be proud of.

In 1989, buying and renovating somewhere in Morocco was far from straightforward. The paperwork and processes were arcane and convoluted, inward investment was far from easy and not everyone understood what they were trying to achieve.

After months of struggle, they managed to gain the approvals necessary. A piece of major luck was meeting up with the architect John Bothamley. His pragmatism, building experience and sense of what was possible in such a remote location made sure that the building was feasible and beautiful, and could work within the challenging restrictions the team had set themselves.

These restrictions were thoughtful. As far as possible local craftsmen undertook the rebuilding of the Kasbah rather than builders brought in from Marrakech. This both provided local employment and maintained local skills. Extensive and ongoing renovation and new building work were undertaken without power tools or modern machinery.

The result is a place to stay that feels unique for the traveller. It has attracted visitors from all over the world, including the British ambassador in Morocco. As a place to stay, it has been featured in the London *Sunday Times* and has won many awards.

The Kasbah is not a conventional hotel, and the accommodation is a mixture of traditional Berber salons and elegant, cool rooms, with furniture and other objects reflecting local ideas and crafts. The food and hospitality are authentically Berber and local traditions and etiquette are maintained. It has become a place not just for the wanderer going on up into the High Atlas Mountains but a place to stop, let go and think. The roof of the Kasbah on which you can sleep provides an environment of almost indescribable tranquillity. All this on its own would make the place remarkable. But the Kasbah is more than an unusual and exotic place to stay, and its commitment to the local community goes beyond providing work for local artisans.

The Kasbah taxes itself 5 per cent of its revenue, which is ploughed back into local community projects. The team have also acted as catalysts in the creation of a Village Association to help local people deal more effectively with regional and national authorities. They also underwrote the purchase of the village's first ambulance and sponsored a driver. Lack of local medical transportation to hospitals considerable distances away in Asni and Marrakech often resulted in unnecessary deaths, for example in childbirth.

Other plans include the provision of English lessons for Kasbah staff and assistance to set up a maternity programme. They have also worked to organise refuse collection. Refuse is a real problem as increasing tourism and the buying in of food and other things that involve large amounts of packaging impact upon a fragile landscape, with no infrastructure to cope.

Larger projects include a safe drinking water system for all the villages of Imlil and a central hammam (steam bath).

Strategically, the Kasbah is very aware of the dangers of the growth in tourism creating an economic monoculture in which vagaries of world travel, such as those resulting from 9/11, can be disastrous. Therefore, the Kasbah directs much of its attention to those projects that will encourage diverse employment and a sustainable future for the villages.

And again, this is not done in a spirit of colonial paternalism but in genuine partnership with the local community. As Mike McHugo told me:

> I imagine such a project would not be possible without close and deep local ties. I also believe that hopefully by our correct behaviour and respect for the local population they have come to respect us and also accept some of our differences. One of the aphorisms we have on the tower of the Kasbah is: 'God shall know them by their deeds', which comes from the Koran.

Audacity – dreaming with your eyes open

The Kasbah is audacious. Its audacity is not born out of the huge resources of a large corporation but because it works at so many different motivational levels. To go there is to see all eight of Michael Apter's 'eight ways of being' expressed in tangible, positive ways. Perhaps the mixture of the McHugos' different worlds enables the Kasbah to remain commercially viable and increasingly successful. It is interesting as this book closes to compare it with The Eden Project: both seem to thrive because they have wilfully defied conventional thinking, while retaining a sound business approach. At the heart of both ventures are values that address funda-mental aspects of ourselves. They are richly appealing.

The Road to Audacity is essentially about rediscovering what it means for work to be based upon what it is to be human, and to make sure that our organisations address and create the conditions in which all aspects of people's personality can flourish.

The focus of this is not an argument about social responsibility but about motivational connection. This connection is the context and powerful underpinning for the undoubted good practice that surrounds us, all those strategic insights and techniques, and the potential for us to defy the uncertainty we try and pretend we can count.

As mentioned earlier, this book was first thought of in one of the towers on the roof of the Kasbah. Although I have been lucky enough to travel all over the world, on that evening as the low glow of a long, hot, dusty day lingered on the sides of the hills, I felt as far away from the uncertainty and confusion of modern life as I ever have. Reflecting upon this, I think I was struck by the coherence of the spirit of this place. It was not discon-nected from everyday reality, it was just connected in a different way – a way in which the dream it has of itself could be fulfilled rather than just wished for.

In this way, I started *The Road to Audacity* at its destination and discov-ered the journey that it might require. Mike Apter speaks powerfully of the values that lie at the heart of each of the motivational states: achievement at the heart of seriousness, enjoyment within playfulness, fitting in prompting a state of conforming, and the spark for freedom that prompts rebelliousness. Mastery gives us access to the value of power and sympathy to love. Our need for separateness is met by the value of indi-viduation, and the need to merge ourselves with others in the value of transcendence – to be part of something greater than ourselves.

Actions that help to meet these needs enable us to build meaning from our experience, developing our sense of self-worth. We are motivated to be audacious when we see that we can meet these values. Motivationally, what we value will change as we move between the states. The mystery of the Kasbah (and I am not the only one to be inspired by it) means that whichever motivational state you are in, you can see its intrinsic value being met in a special and more profound way. These places are very effective at nourishing, inspiring and appealing to the forces – the eight ways of being – that motivate us and affect our behaviour.

Organisationally, this level of inspiration may not be something that every organisation wants or needs to achieve, although it is a curious thing for people not to want to be inspired. But organisations who want generally to develop a greater level of engagement with the people that work for them or buy from them, and specifically to become more audacious, might consider very carefully the climate or environment they create and how these fundamental personal values are nurtured. A light should be turned on the real organisational values that exist – how do they support and reflect the more individual values?

An audacious organisation in particular is a place in which the journey, the unknown and a struggle – possibly involving enjoyment, freedom and power – can all be achieved.

This is an ambitious vision. I hear a cynical laugh. Laugh again, but audacious organisations dream with their eyes open – and wouldn't you rather work for one?

INDEX